Oscar Loew

The Physiological Role of Mineral Nutrients

Oscar Loew

The Physiological Role of Mineral Nutrients

ISBN/EAN: 9783743325210

Manufactured in Europe, USA, Canada, Australia, Japa

Cover: Foto ©ninafisch / pixelio.de

Manufactured and distributed by brebook publishing software
(www.brebook.com)

Oscar Loew

The Physiological Role of Mineral Nutrients

BULLETIN No. 18.

V. P. P.—68.

U. S. DEPARTMENT OF AGRICULTURE.

DIVISION OF VEGETABLE PHYSIOLOGY AND PATHOLOGY.

B. T. GALLOWAY, CHIEF.

THE

PHYSIOLOGICAL RÔLE OF MINERAL NUTRIENTS.

BY

OSCAR LOEW,

OF THE

Division of Vegetable Physiology and Pathology

WASHINGTON:

GOVERNMENT PRINTING OFFICE.

1899.

LETTER OF TRANSMITTAL.

U. S. Department of Agriculture,
Division of Vegetable Physiology and Pathology,
Washington, D. C., September 28, 1899.

Sir: I respectfully transmit herewith a bulletin prepared by Dr. Oscar Loew, of this Division, on the physiological rôle of mineral nutrients. For several years Dr. Loew has been engaged in the study of the functions of mineral nutrients in plants. This work has led into new fields, and has resulted in discoveries which it is believed will be of much practical value to agriculture. The importance of mineral nutrients is so well known as to need little comment, but the part each plays in the life of an organism is still largely a matter of conjecture. It is evident that we can not hope to understand nutrition until we become better acquainted with the physiological action of the nutrients themselves. The main object of this bulletin is to show what has been accomplished in this direction, and to encourage and stimulate work along the lines laid down. The matter has been prepared primarily for teachers and experiment station workers, and is therefore treated from a technical rather than a practical standpoint. I respectfully recommend that it be published as Bulletin No. 18 of this Division.

Respectfully,

B. T. Galloway,
Chief of Division.

Hon. James Wilson,
Secretary of Agriculture.

2

CONTENTS.

3

4

THE PHYSIOLOGICAL RÔLE OF MINERAL NUTRIENTS.

By Oscar Loew.

GENERAL REMARKS ON THE MINERAL CONSTITUENTS FOUND IN ORGANISMS.

HISTORICAL NOTES.

The functions of the mineral nutrients in plants and animals constitute a highly important problem. Normal development is impeded by the decrease and entirely prevented by the absence of even a single nutrient, and gradual decline, disease, and finally death will result from the continued withholding of any such substance. Thus yellow spots will develop on the leaves of the sugar beet when the soil is deficient in lime; mold fungi will not develop spores but only mycelium when the amount of magnesia in the nourishing medium becomes too small; and even the primary segmentation will stop entirely in the fecundated eggs of lower marine animals when lime salts are withheld, while every further physiological action comes to an end as soon as sodium salts are substituted for potassium salts in the cells. Pigeons die in a few weeks when fed with materials too poor in mineral matter, and dogs can not subsist on meat which has been macerated with cold water, by which means most of the mineral matter is removed. The result of eating such food is weakness of the muscles and nervous excitability, which finally lead to death with spasms and the symptoms of suffocation.

In examining highly differentiated plants and animals there are observed not only certain differences as to the total sum of mineral matter in the different organs of the same organism, but also certain regularities as to the proportions of the mineral constituents. On the other hand, pathological conditions lead to a partial excretion of the mineral matter. Thus, in tuberculosis of man the excretion of lime and magnesia is increased, and in diabetes the increased excretion of lime is a specific symptom. These facts can be understood properly only when it is admitted that for the normal functions of normal organs a certain amount of lime and magnesia is indispensable.

5

Humphrey Davy [1] was the first savant to consider the mineral constituents essential for the development of plants. He says: "The chemistry of the simpler manures (the manures which act in very small quantities, such as gypsum, alkalies, and various saline substances), has hitherto been exceedingly obscure. It has been generally supposed that these materials act in the vegetable economy in the same manner as condiments or stimulants in the animal economy, and that they render the common food more nutritive. It seems, however, a much more probable idea that they are actually a part of the true food of plants, and that they supply that kind of matter to the vegetable fiber which is analogous to the bony matter in animal structures." Davy mentions among other things the beneficial action of gypsum, bone dust, and slaked lime. Indeed, the favorable effects of wood ash, bone dust, and liming upon vegetation have been known since olden times. Furthermore, mills for grinding bones existed early in this century in France and England, and enterprising men went so far as to dig up battlefields in Europe and unearth thousands of tons of bones for agricultural purposes.

Sprengel [2] was the second one to express an opinion on this subject. He says: "We can accept it as an indisputable fact that mineral matters found in plants also are real nutrients for them, and that it is not their action upon the humus which makes them important, since gypsum, potassium sulphate, and calcium phosphate do not at all act upon the humus." [3]

In quite a different sense Berzelius argued the same year that the action of lime is simply that of a stimulant for the plant and a solvent for the humus, while lime and alkali promote the rotting of organic materials, as manure.

After Sprengel followed Liebig (1840), whose theories received substantial support in the important researches of Wiegmann and Polstorf (1842). However, great as was Liebig's merit in overthrowing the dominant theory of the nourishing qualities of organic matter, called humus, in the soil, and in showing the absolute necessity of mineral salts in plants, the fact can not be denied that he made various errors, especially in his earlier years. For instance, he at one time believed that mineral bases serve merely to neutralize the organic acids in the plant and that they could replace each other, and further, that alkaloids in plants could play the part of mineral bases. He ascribed certain

[1] Elements of Agricultural Chemistry, London, 1814.
[2] Theorie der Düngung, 1839.
[3] As a significant fact it may be mentioned that the Prussian Academy of Sciences, in the year 1800 offered a prize for an investigation to decide whether the mineral matters found in plants are taken up from the soil or whether they are produced in the plants themselves by vital power. This question was treated by Schrader, whose decision was in favor of the latter opinion. How much farther advanced was Saussure, who, in 1804, declared that the mineral matter of humus contribute in a certain degree to its fertility, since the same are found in the ashes of the plants (Récherches sur la végétation).

diseases of plants solely to the deficiency of mineral matter in the soil, but later investigations have demonstrated that fungous or animal parasites are the true causes. After about twenty years of hard fighting the importance of Liebig's mineral theory was in the main recognized and the old humus theory abandoned. However, his opinion that the mineral bases replace each other has been proved to be erroneous by the experiments of Wolff, Knop, Hellriegel, and others. The indispensability of potassa was proved, especially by Friedrich Nobbe, Schroeder, and Erdmann (1871), as was also the noxious character of lithium salts for Phanerogams. But the real significance of the bases in the plant cells has not been cleared up, and, as a botanist has expressed it, the solution of these problems must form an important final goal for every plant physiologist.

When Liebig had called attention to the necessity of certain mineral constituents in plants he set his assistants and students at work to analyze the ashes of a great number of plants. He published an account of these analyses in his works on agriculture, but a more comprehensive review on plant ashes is given in the tables of E. Wolff.[1]

These results show that the quantitative composition of the ash of one and the same plant varies according to the soil upon which it is grown, but that qualitatively there is no difference. This observation, which led Liebig to erroneous assumptions, was properly explained much later. It was found that every plant absolutely requires a certain minimum of each mineral nutrient, and that in most cases besides this minimum it takes up not only an excess of these various compounds, but also substances which are perhaps useful but not absolutely necessary for plant functions, such as sodium salts and silica. In the case of potassium or calcium salts a moderate surplus is not noxious. A large excess of lime taken up can be easily excluded from secondary influences by transformation into oxalate or carbonate—salts which are often produced by plants. Plants adapted to saline desert soils show incrustations on their leaves, which may sometimes contain, in addition to chlorid, nitrate, and sulphate of sodium, more than 50 per cent of calcium carbonate.

The surplus of mineral matter found in plants—nutrient as well as indifferent compounds—depends to a great extent upon the intensity of the current of transpiration, which explains why herbaceous plants show a higher percentage of ash for the dry matter than do the leaves of woody plants. While cabbage leaves, which have about 90 per cent water, contain 15 to 18 per cent ash for the dry matter, the leaves of potatoes, clover, and grass, having 78 to 80 per cent water, contain only 6 to 9 per cent ash for the dry matter. In trees adapted to moist soil, for instance, *Salix*, *Populus*, *Acer*, and *Tilia*, the leaves contain more water and also generally more ash for the dry matter than do the leaves of trees in which transpiration goes on more slowly, such as *Quercus*,

[1] Aschen Analysen (2 volumes), Berlin, 1871 and 1880.

Fagus, and the common kinds of *Pinus*. While leaves of *Acer* show 7 to 9 per cent of ash and those of *Salix* 4 to 6 per cent, the leaves of *Pinus montana* and *P. austriaca* show only 0.58 per cent and 0.74 per cent, respectively (Ebermayer). There is more ash in the leaves than in the roots or stems, more in the roots and stems than in the seeds, and more in the seeds than in the wood.

ECOLOGICAL AND PHYSIOLOGICAL RÔLE OF MINERAL SUBSTANCES.

A question of fundamental importance is whether a certain mineral constituent has one or several functions to perform, and in the latter case whether at least one of these several functions may not be performed by some other related constituent—in other words, whether a partial substitution in the organisms would be possible. When a mere neutralization of acids or an osmotic action is involved there can be no doubt that potassa or lime may be replaced by soda, or when incrustation of a tissue is necessary for protection the place of calcium carbonate might be taken even by silica. The solution of various mineral salts produces osmotic pressure and motion required also by animals. Thus beef tea containing 0.35 gram of salts per liter, exerts an osmotic energy of several atmospheres, of which, however, only about one-fourth can be realized in the stomach, since the blood itself also contains mineral salts. However, it suffices to produce an aqueous current from the blood to the stomach, while in the intestines the current takes the opposite direction.[1] Such functions are not specific, however. But in the purely physiological functions of a chemical nature not even a partial substitution is possible, notwithstanding that various assertions have been made to the contrary. The most novel supposition in connection with this idea of substitution, and one very amusing to chemists, is that seriously made in a recent text-book of plant physiology, that is, that on other planets there may exist living organisms in which the carbon of the organic matter is replaced by silicon.

In order to furnish a foundation upon which to base a theory of the special functions of the various mineral constituents, separate analyses for each kind of organ are indispensable. In former times entire plants or animals were subjected to incineration and the ash analyzed, but such results were of very restricted value.[2] A distinction may be drawn between ecological and physiological functions. In the former case the mineral compound serves either as a mechanical support of the organic forms, as does for example the calcium phosphate in the case of bones, and probably the silica in grasses, feathers,[3] and hair; or it furnishes a protection against noxious influences from the outside, and against the attacks of enemies,[4] as do the needle crystals of calcium

---

[1] Köppe, Therap. Monatshefte, 1897.

[2] Thus one author has inferred from his analyses that there is less magnesia in cats and dogs and less potassa in dogs than in rabbits (Zeitschr. Biol., Vol. X, p. 321).

[3] The organic silica compound in feathers was recently studied by Drechsel.

[4] It has been asserted that the siliceous deposit in the bark of *Fagus* and *Acer* and in the leaves of various other plants forms a protection against parasitic fungi.

oxalate in certain leaves against snails; the incrustations of leaves and entire plants (Chara) by calcium carbonate; the lime shells of *Foraminifera*, certain worms, mollusca, and eggs of birds; the silica shells of diatoms; and the secretion of dilute sulphuric acid by certain *Gastropoda*, as *Dolium*, *Cassis*, etc. Finally, mineral matter may be an object of adaptation, as the salts in sea water is for marine animals. However, in this bulletin the physiological rôle alone is the subject of discussion.

MINERAL COMPOUNDS FOUND IN ORGANISMS.

The mineral compounds usually found in living organisms are phosphates, sulphates, carbonates, chlorids, silica, iron compounds, magnesia, lime, soda, and potassa; while in plants nitrates, manganic compounds, and minute quantities of fluorides also often occur. Small quantities of iodine compounds are found in both kingdoms. Bromine compounds occur in sea weeds. Occasionally there are present in plants small quantities of titanic and boracic acids, lithia, and alumina, and of the oxids of lead, zinc, and copper.[1] Sodium salts are not necessary for physiological uses of plants, but are for those of animals. Calcium salts are of great importance for plants and animals, only the lower fungi and lower algæ being able to do without them. Magnesium and potassium salts, however, can not be dispensed with by any living cell any more than can phosphoric acid. Manganese, which was shown by Risse to be incapable of replacing the iron in plants and was believed to be entirely useless, forms, according to recent researches of Bertrand, an essential constituent of the vegetable oxidizing enzyms, and hence may be also of physiological interest.[2] The nitrates and sulphates present in plants serve, in regard to their acids, chiefly as sources of nitrogen and sulphur for protein formation, and consequently do not require further discussion. As physiological elements these must be designated potassium, sodium, calcium, magnesium, iron, phosphorus, chlorine, iodine, carbon, hydrogen, nitrogen, oxygen, and sulphur.

GENERAL VALUE OF CERTAIN MINERAL SALTS.

Mineral salts have not only to perform ecological as well as specific chemical functions, but also seem to contribute directly to the maintenance of the continuance of the living condition of the protoplasm. A most striking instance of this is the rapid dying of infusoria in distilled water. The writer entertained for a time the supposition that this

---

[1] Lippmann observed in the sugar beet not only boric acid and copper oxid, but also traces of vanadin and cæsium compounds (Bot. Jahrb., 1888). Wait found 0.31 per cent titanic acid in the ash of oak wood, 0.11 per cent in the ash of apples, and traces of it in bones and meat, and Dunnington found it in many soils.

[2] According to Lepinois, iron can replace manganese in this regard, and the formation of oxidase in plants raised in the absence of manganese was further observed by Albert F. Woods.

phenomenon might be due, as in the case of the alga *Spirogyra*, to slight traces of copper sometimes found in distilled water and derived from the copper vessels used in distilling. Experiments were therefore repeated, water distilled from glass vessels being used, but the effect was the same—the infusoria died with bloating, their protoplasm swelling and disintegrating. The only conclusion that can be drawn, therefore, is that the distilled water extracts from them traces of necessary constituents, which must be of mineral nature, since common water containing some mineral matter has no such action, but forms the very medium of existence for these organisms. A similar effect could not be observed with the same distilled water on algæ cells, which may remain alive in it for a considerable time, although the growth ceases. But here the walls of the cytoplasm are probably of greater density, which would prevent the mineral matters of the cell from passing easily to the outside.

This phenomenon observed in the case of infusoria strongly resembles. that of the red blood corpuscles and leucocytes, which are adapted to the degree of concentration of the serum, and which die when transferred into distilled water, but remain alive for some time in a sodium chlorid solution of 0.6 per cent. The nature of the mineral salts loosely bound by the proteids of the living matter may vary with the character of these proteids. In the one case it may be sodium chlorid, in another the secondary potassium phosphate, and in a third a calcium salt. It should be pointed out once for all that we can hope to understand the living state of protoplasm only when the proteins of the living matter are recognized to be chemically labil bodies, which the slightest influence often suffices to transform into the more stable isomeric forms of dead matter. Relatively stable proteins are also those in milk and the reserve proteins in eggs and seeds. Spontaneous transformations of labil compounds into stable ones by atomic migration often take place very easily, for example, when certain amido aldehydes or amido ketones are liberated from their combination with acids.

Years ago M. Nencki[1] recognized the importance of the mineral matter combined with the plasma proteids. "All proteins[2] occurring in the living organisms are combined with mineral substances, whereby the proteins concerned acquire specific properties and functional significance in the organisms."

It may be proper here to call attention to another phenomenon, first recognized by Wolff. He determined the minimum of each mineral nutrient necessary for the normal development of the oat plant when the other mineral nutrients were in excess, and found that when all the mineral nutrients are offered in the determined minimum amounts at the same time it is impossible for the plants to flower and fruit

[1] Arch. des. Sci. Biologiques de St. Petersburg. 1894, Vol. III, p. 312.

[2] While "protein" is the general denomination of all kinds of albuminous substances, the word "proteid" applies especially to the complex proteins, e. g., nucleo-albumin, mucin, hæmoglobin, etc.

normally. When only the absolutely necessary minimum of one of the nutrients is offered a certain surplus of some of the others must be present.

THE LOW ATOMIC WEIGHT OF THE MINERAL NUTRIENTS.

A review of the elements necessary for organic life shows at once that they have low atomic weights, iron, with an atomic weight of 56, having the highest among them. This is due, according to Leo Errera, not only to their more frequent occurrence in the various compounds making up the earth's crust, but also to their higher specific heat. Thus water, constituting as a rule two-thirds to three-fourths and sometimes even more of the weight of a living organism, has the highest specific heat of all substances, consequently it can diminish the effects of rapidly changing temperatures upon life.

THE PHYSIOLOGICAL RÔLE OF PHOSPHORIC ACID.

RELATION OF PHOSPHORIC ACID TO PROTEIDS AND TO THE DIVISION OF CELLS.

Phosphoric acid is, above all, necessary for the formation of lecithin[1] and the nucleo proteids, e. g., chromatin[2] and plastin—the most essential constituents of the nucleus and plastids. This makes clear the statement of former writers, that phosphoric acid "follows the proteids," since every new cell requires them. Wherever phosphoric acid is transformed from the dissolved condition to an insoluble compound, as in the formation and growth of the nucleus, fresh quantities must move thither, according to the law of diffusion. The embryos can develop by cell division only when phosphates are stored up in sufficient quantities in the seeds for the formation and increase of the nuclear substance in the new cells. Phosphoric acid, further, is not only contained as calcium and magnesium phosphate in the globoids, but is also distributed in the seeds as dipotassium phosphate.

The observation that the total mass of protein in seeds is increased by an increased supply of phosphoric acid would also be easily understood on the basis of the hypothesis of Strasburger and Schmitz that the nuclei are the manufacturers of the protein matter. This hypothesis is highly probable, and in fact has been confirmed by Hofer in the case of enzyms,[3] which must be considered as a class of proteins.

---

[1] Two other phosphoric acid compounds, which are, however, restricted to the higher animals, are jecorin and inosic acid, the latter probably being merely a product of metabolism. Besides phosphoric acid, the latter yields on decomposition hypoxanthin and probably trioxyvalerianic acid (Heuser). Another compound, thus far encountered in plants only, yields, besides phosphoric acid among other things, inosite (Schulze and Winterstein).

[2] The nuclein extracted from organized structures is essentially an altered chromatin.

[3] Sitzungsberichte der Morph. Physiol. Ges., München, 1889.

In order to observe how a deficiency of phosphoric acid would interfere with the normal action of plant cells the writer compared at a low temperature the behavior of algæ (*Spirogyra*) in complete culture solutions[1] with that of algæ cultivated for eight weeks in solutions free from phosphoric acid, but containing all other necessary mineral nutrients. The result was that there was no growth in the absence of the phosphoric acid, but there was a yellow coloration of the chlorophyll and an accumulation of fat and albumin, while in the control algæ the number of cells had more than doubled, the coloration of the chlorophyll was normal, and the amount of fat and albumin stored up was much smaller than in the former case. When, however, at the end of eight weeks, 0.1 per mille of monopotassium phosphate was added to the culture free from phosphoric acid, a most energetic cell division began in most of the cells after a short time, thus demonstrating the great importance of phosphoric acid for this purpose.

A direct participation of inorganic phosphates in the formation of · albumin, as Liebig had assumed, has not been proved, and is improbable. As the writer has observed, cells of algæ can continue to form albumin for a certain length of time, even in the absence of inorganic phosphates, although further growth and multiplication will thus be stopped.[2]

THE PHYSIOLOGICAL IMPORTANCE OF LECITHIN.

This ester of phosphoric acid contains fatty acids, glycerol, phosphoric acid, and choline, and corresponds to the following formula:[3]

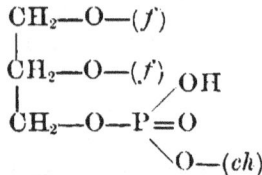

$$
\begin{array}{l}
CH_2-O-(f) \\
CH_2-O-(f)\diagdown_{OH} \\
CH_2-O-P=O \\
\qquad\qquad\diagdown_{O-(ch)}
\end{array}
$$

It is a regular concomitant of fatty matter. It swells up in water and is even somewhat soluble in it, a property which renders it physiologically superior to the ordinary fatty matter. The chief function of lecithin is probably to serve for respiration; it represents the form into

---

[1] The composition of the solution made with distilled water was as follows for the control culture :

	Per mille.
Potassium nitrate	0.2
Calcium nitrate	0.2
Sodium sulphate	0.1
Magnesium sulphate	0.1
Monopotassium phosphate	0.1
Ferrous sulphate	Trace.

The monopotassium phosphate was left out in one of the solutions.

[2] Biol. Centralbl., 1891, Vol. IX, No. 9.

[3] (f) Signifies the radical of a higher fatty acid; (ch) signifies the radical of choline.

which the fat must be changed to become combustible in the proto-plasm, since the substances serving for respiration, must be present in the protoplasm in a dissolved condition.[1] Since fat is not soluble, a transformation of it into soap was formerly assumed—a view which is hardly possible in the case of plants, while upon animals soaps injected subcutaneously exert a poisonous action (Munk, 1889).

By the transformation of fatty matter into lecithin the higher fatty acids are offered to the protoplasm in a soluble form, and after being oxidized other molecules of fatty acids may enter into the place of the former and thus the same molecules of the glycerol-phosphoric acid can serve repeatedly as vehicles for oxidations of molecules of fatty acids. The fact that blood corpuscles contain lecithin. but not fat seems to indicate that lecithin may be produced not only from fat, but also directly from sugar, as is fat. A great therapeutic value of lecithin has been demonstrated in cases of nervous debility and weakness of the alimentary functions. The brain and the whole nervous system in general are rich in lecithin, fully 17 per cent of it having been found in the gray substance of the brain. The nervous system requires for its perpetual great activity a substance which unites easy combusti-bility with a great deal of potential energy in a small volume, which conditions are admirably united in the lecithin.

Seeds rich in starch generally contain much less lecithin than those rich in protein. Thus barley grains contain less than half the amount contained in soy beans. The amount of lecithin increases to a certain point in the first stages of germination, while the amount of fat decreases.[2] Here the lecithin is evidently formed from the fat. It seems very probable that the observed increase of lecithin is less than was actually formed, since a part of it is probably consumed nearly as quickly as produced. The evergreen tea leaves lose the reserve lecithin in spring (Hanai) and green plants generally lose it when kept in the dark (Stoklasa). Heffter observed a decrease in the amount of lecithin in the liver during starvation. E. Schulze[3] found that during germi-nation the quantity of choline increases, and that in wheat the choline is localized in the germ of the grain, but not in the endosperm. This is certainly of physiological interest, since the young developing germ must carry on an energetic respiration and therefore be capable of easily forming lecithin, in which process the presence of choline is required. It may further be mentioned in this connection that, accord-ing to Müntz, the amount of free fatty acids increases during germina-tion, which is to be expected when lecithin is formed from fat. From

---

[1] We can observe this with cholesterin, which is frequently contained in the cells and in fact is, like lecithin, a constant concomitant of fatty matter. It is not per-ceptibly oxidized by the protoplasm, the almost absolute insolubility in water being here the obstacle.

[2] Maxwell, Chem. Centralbl., Vol. XLI, No. 1, p. 365; Frankfurt, Landw. Vers. Stat., Vol. XLIII.

[3] Landw. Vers. Stat., Vol. XLVI.

all the observations cited it will be seen that lecithin plays an important rôle, and as its formation is made possible only when phosphoric acid is present, one of the functions of this acid at once becomes intelligible.

PHOSPHORIC ACID IN CHLOROPHYLL.

As Trécul, Gautier, and Hoppe have shown, the crystallized chlorophyllan also contains phosphoric acid (1.39 per cent)—indeed, for the formation of the chlorophyll green the presence of phosphoric acid is absolutely required (see p. 16). The opinion has been expressed that the crystallized chlorophyllan is a kind of lecithin. While it is the orthophosphoric acid that is contained in lecithin and chlorophyll, it is the metaphosphoric acid which forms a constituent of the chromatin (nuclein), as Leo Liebermann has discovered.

POTASSIUM PHOSPHATE AS A CELL CONSTITUENT.

That the secondary potassium phosphate as such also has an important physiological function becomes probable from its general occurrence in the living organisms. Relatively large proportions of it are found in yeast cells, in the forming seeds, in the liver and muscles, and in fact in all cases where special demands for great chemical achievements are made. It causes the weak alkaline reaction of protoplasm and is probably present in loose combination with certain proteins, from which even treatment with water will often easily remove most of it.

The dry substance of muscles contains about 4 per cent of mineral matter, of which again nearly two-thirds consist of dipotassium phosphate. This is also nearly the proportion found in beer yeast. Wheat grains contain from 1 to 2 per cent ash, of which nearly one-half consists of potassium phosphate and nearly one-fourth of calcium and magnesium phosphate, while another portion of phosphoric acid present in that ash corresponds to the destroyed nuclein and to the small portion of lecithin.[1]

A further special function of phosphoric acid is the use of calcium phosphate for the formation of bones. The blood ash of cattle contains 4 to 6 per cent and of man 9 to 11 per cent of phosphoric acid. The requirements for normal field crops are considerable, a wheat crop, for example, extracting from 1 hectare (about 2.5 acres) of ground about 26.5 kilos of this acid. The forest products require much less. It is in the production of seeds especially that the powerful influence of fertilization with phosphates becomes apparent.

Whether hypophosphites, phosphites, or hypophosphates can ever be of physiological value is a question which must be determined by further studies. Knop showed in an experiment with maize in 1881

[1] Several views have been expressed as to the transportation of calcium phosphate to the seeds. This salt is insoluble in water, but may be dissolved in small quantities by the weak acid juices of the plant. Vaudin (Chem. Zeit., No. 91, 1895) believes that its transportation in the vegetable organism is accomplished by sugar and potassium malate or citrate, which dissolve it in small quantities.

that phosphoric acid can not be replaced by hypophosphoric acid. The writer has observed that algæ are at least not injured by a 1 per mille solution of sodium hypophosphite, phosphite, or pyro and meta phosphate, and the two last-mentioned salts can even be well utilized by mold fungi.[1] The assertion once made that phosphoric acid in algæ may be replaced by arsenic acid is absurd and moreover Molisch had shown it to be impossible.

THE PHYSIOLOGICAL RÔLE OF IRON COMPOUNDS.

RELATION BETWEEN THE COLORING MATTER OF THE BLOOD AND OF THE LEAF.

Iron compounds are indispensable for the production of the chlorophyll[2] of the plant and the hæmoglobin of the red blood corpuscles of the higher animals. Without the former there is no assimilation of carbonic acid, hence no synthesis of organic matter in the green plant, and without the latter no respiration of the vertebrates, since it is the hæmoglobin that carries the molecular oxygen to the remotest regions of the body. Although the chlorophyll itself does not contain iron, hæmoglobin contains it as an essential constituent in the molecule.

There is evidently a close relation between the coloring matter of the leaf and that of the blood. The phylloporphyrin obtained from chlorophyll by the action of alkalies shows almost the same spectrum as the hæmatoporphyrin obtained from the hæmoglobin of the blood. Hæmatoporphyrin seems to correspond to a dioxyphylloporphyrin, and both of these compounds appear to be derivatives of pyrrol. It was especially the investigations of Nencki and of Tschirch that first directed attention to the analogies between these two physiologically important bodies.

INFLUENCE OF IRON AND OTHER MINERAL NUTRIENTS ON THE FORMATION OF CHLOROPHYLL.

Iron is not the only requisite for the production of chlorophyll. Other mineral nutrients are not less necessary, and above all only a normal plastid can produce the green color with the aid of iron salts and thus become a chloroplast; hence cases of imperfect plastids may occur, e. g., where an increased supply of lime is required to produce normally green leaves. A case where phosphoric acid was required in addition to the iron to produce the chlorophyll was observed by the writer in the case of an alga. Some threads of *Spirogyra majuscula* were placed

---

[1] Bot. Centralbl., 1895.

[2] An observation on chlorophyll made by the writer may here be mentioned, as it places the great sensibility of this substance toward chemical reagents beyond a doubt. When *Spirogyra* threads are treated with moderately concentrated hydrochloric acid, they at once assume a yellowish color, but soon afterwards turn to a bluish green, which points to two successive changes and indicates that in the preparation of pure chlorophyll strong acids have to be avoided. Various discrepancies in the observations of different authors may be traced to this circumstance.

in 2 liters of distilled water, to which were added only 0.2 per mille calcium nitrate and 0.02 per mille ammonium sulphate. When they were placed in this very imperfect solution, the filaments contained in all probability some stored-up mineral matter, hence a moderate further growth of the cells was not surprising. Besides, mineral matter of some cells which died gradually may have been absorbed by the living ones. The cells did not increase by cell division, however, but merely enlarged. After standing six weeks the chlorophyll bodies had assumed a yellow color. The liquid, with the filaments, after the addition of 0.02 per mille ferrous sulphate, was now divided into two portions, and 0.5 per mille secondary sodium phosphate was added to one of them. After five days a very striking difference was noticed, the normal green reappearing only in the latter case, which proved that phosphoric acid is an essential factor for the production of chlorophyll. Stoklasa also has observed the necessity of phosphoric acid for the production of the chlorophyll green, and finally Macchiata[1] inferred from his experiments that plants may become chlorotic not only from a deficiency of iron, but also from lack of other mineral nutrients. Indeed, cases exist in which it is the deficiency of magnesia which causes this phenomenon (p. 49). Magnesia appears to form a constituent of the crystallized chlorophyllan of Hoppe, which, however, has recently been declared a mixture[2] which contains 1.72 per cent ash, of which 1.38 parts are phosphoric acid (mentioned above) and 0.34 magnesia (Hoppe).

An interesting fact observed by Zimmermann[3] is that the chloroplasts in chlorotic leaves are smaller than in normal leaves, and appear to be incapable of forming starch from sugar. Different from chlorosis is the albinism of plants. Here the leucoplasts have so far degenerated that they become incapable of producing the green color even when all the necessary mineral nutrients are present. Although incapable of forming carbohydrates from carbonic acid, however, they often form starch from sugar.[1]

FERTILIZING EFFECT OF IRON SALTS.

It is to be expected that a moderate manuring with iron salts would prove beneficial for plants grown on soil deficient in iron. Bracci[4] mixed 1 part of ferrous sulphate with 20 parts of silt and applied this mixture to soil in which oats and wheat were grown, and as a result the grain ripened several days earlier and the yields of straw and grain were increased. Spraying with ferrous sulphate is also said to produce favorable results. Ville applied a 2 per cent solution to young apple and pear fruits,[5] and thus not only hastened the ripening

---

[1] Bot. Jahresber., 1888, p. 20.
[2] Compare also the recent publications of Schunk and Marchlewski.
[3] Zimmermann, Beiträge zur Morph., etc., Heft II; Sapoznikoff, Bot. C., 1889, p. 321.
[4] Bot. Jahresber., 1883, p. 43.
[5] Ibid, p. 14. Other reports, however, mention an injurious action of a 1 per cent solution upon potato plants.

process, but also enlarged the size of the fruit. Cugini tries to explain this on the ground of stimulation of the protoplasm and increased production of chloroplasts in the epidermis.

ORGANIC COMPOUNDS CONTAINING IRON.

Hæmoglobin is not the only organic iron compound in organisms. Bunge isolated from the yolk of eggs a nuclein-like body, hæmatogen, which contained 5 per cent phosphorus and 0.23 per cent iron, and similar substances were observed by Zaleski in the liver of animals and by Macallum and Stoklasa in the nuclei of plant cells. Spitzer found in animals oxidizing enzyms, which were nucleo-proteids containing about 0.2 per cent of iron.

IRON IN FUNGI.

The question as to whether iron salts are necessary for fungi was formerly answered in the negative. Molisch,[1] however, observed that even very small traces of iron salts have a great effect upon the growth of fungi, and having discovered traces of it in the ash of various fungi, he considers it a necessary element for them. Indeed, slight traces of iron are frequently present in the nutrient compounds used for the cultivation of fungi. Certain writers admit that iron produces a beneficial effect, but deny that it is absolutely necessary. However, Molisch's observation that in fungi iron can not be replaced by nickel, cobalt, manganese, or zinc deserves special consideration. Traces of zinc and related salts will, according to Raulin, Ono, and Richards, also increase the fungus mass in a given time. Richards has shown that the nutrients are more economically disposed of under this influence. It may also be mentioned here that Gautier and Drouin observed that ferric oxid promotes the fixation of atmospheric nitrogen by soil bacteria.[2]

MANGANESE IN PLANTS.

Physiologically, manganese can not replace iron in plants. Plants have also been raised to perfection in culture solutions which contained no trace of manganese. However, the ash of plants, especially of woody ones, sometimes contains even more manganese than iron. Schroeder calculated for 1 hectare of eighty year old beech trees near Tharand a content of 104.1 kilos of Mn_3O_4, but only a content of 7.92 kilos of Fe_2O_3[3]. The ash of *Pinus strobus* showed a content of 2.06 per cent Mn_3O_4, and that of *Populus tremula* 1.06 per cent Mn_3O_4 (Weber).

In the case of pines, even the pollen grains contain manganese. Ramann found in them 5.23 per cent ash, and in 100 parts of this ash 1.95 per cent ferric oxid and 1.12 per cent manganic oxid (Mn_3O_4).[4]

[1] Sitzungsber. d. Wien Akad., 1892, Vol. CIII. Aso found nearly 5 per cent ferric oxid in the ash of the spores of *Aspergillus oryzæ*.

[2] Bot. Jahresber., 1888, p. 29.

[3] Wolff's Aschen Analysen, Vol. II.

[4] The manganese content in oxidizing enzyms has been mentioned on p. 9

THE PHYSIOLOGICAL RÔLE OF HALOGEN COMPOUNDS.

PLANTS RAISED WITHOUT CHLORIDS.

The chlorine compounds to be considered in this connection are essentially those of sodium and potassium.[1] These chlorids are not necessary in the physiological functions of lower organisms. Fungi and fresh-water algæ can be successfully cultivated without a trace of a chlorid. In the case of the higher plants, Knop and Batalin successfully cultivated even halophytes in the absence of sodium chlorid, and Knop[2] maintains that chlorids are superfluous for all plants, and hence recommends a culture fluid free from chlorids.[3] On the other hand, functions appear, in certain plants at least, which perhaps by adaptation become dependent upon the presence of chlorine, especially in the form of potassium chlorid.

VALUE OF POTASSIUM CHLORID FOR BUCKWHEAT.

Nobbe has observed that buckwheat plants thrive normally in culture solutions without chlorids until the flowering period is over, but that soon thereafter the tips of the stalks die off; the upper part of the stalk thickens and shows ring-like swellings; the epidermis bursts vertically; the dark green leaves become brittle, spotted, and puffy, and roll in; no fruit is produced;[4] and a microscopical examination shows a great accumulation of starch granules in parts of the stems. These observations have been confirmed by Leydhecker.[5]

It might be supposed that the formation of diastase is prevented by the absence of chlorids, and that the transportation of starch thus becomes impossible, but the difficulty interposed by this hypothesis is that the development of the plant proceeds normally for a considerable length of time, that is, until the flowering stage is reached. This also militates against Detmer's belief that the beneficial action of potassium chlorid on the migration of starch is due to the formation of hydrochloric acid from this chlorid,[6] which acid he claims will in very small quantities promote the saccharification of starch by diastase.

---

[1] Calcium and magnesium chlorid have an injurious effect on plants, probably on account of the liberation of hydrochloric acid in cells, this not being assimilated like nitric or sulphuric acids and therefore accumulating to a noxious degree.

[2] Kreislauf des Stoffs, Vol. I, p. 616. The writer can testify that when 0.01 per cent of sodium or potassium chlorid is added to suitable complete culture solutions no essential difference in growth or the amount of starch will be noticed in the cells of *Spirogyra*, but 0.5 per cent will retard growth.

[3] In Knop's culture fluid the proportion of the mineral nutrients is as follows: 1 KNO₃, 1 KH₂PO₄, 1 MgSO₄, and 4 Ca(NO₃)₂. The iron is suspended as ferric phosphate.

[4] All these phenomena have been observed by the writer in the case of buckwheat plants which received rubidium nitrate, and to a smaller degree also when rubidium chorid was used (p. 24).

[5] Landw. Vers. Stat., 1865 and 1866. Vols. VII and VIII.

[6] Pflanzenphysiol. Unters. über Fermentbildung, Jena, 1884.

INJURIOUS EFFECTS OF CHLORIDS ON PLANTS.

However necessary may be the presence of a certain amount of a chlorid for buckwheat and probably for many other plants, very undesirable results are produced when it is increased beyond a certain point, owing to the fact that the solution of starch might be facilitated in organs the value of which depends on their starch content, as in potatoes. Should it prove to be correct that the chlorids favor the formation of cellulose from sugar, then the decrease of the sugar content in the sugar beet on account of the influence of chlorids would also be explained. On the strength of this hypothesis it might also be inferred that woody growth would be increased by supplying trees with moderate doses of chlorids.

To decide the physiological value of chlorids, plants of other families should also be cultivated in the presence of an abundance of potassium nitrate alone and in combination with potassium chlorid and sodium chlorid. Beyer's[1] experiments with peas and oats are not convincing in this regard, as anyone must infer who compares the composition of his main and control solutions.

An increase of sodium chlorid beyond a certain point has a retarding influence upon assimilation in the chloroplasts (Schimper). Coupin[2] has determined for several plants the amounts that would be injurious; e. g., a solution of 1 per cent will retard the growth of wheat and a solution of 1.8 per cent will prevent its germination. Sodium chlorid reduces the amount of chlorophyll in plants of the seacoast region, but causes the leaves to increase in thickness. The intensity of assimilation of carbonic acid is less in plants on the seacoast than in such plants growing farther inland (Griffon). Certain algæ, such as *Spirogyra crassa*, will suffer in culture solutions containing 0.5 per cent potassium or sodium chlorid, while lower kinds are not affected by 1 per cent chlorid of sodium or even more, and certain bacteria and small yeasts can even grow in the presence of from 10 to 12 per cent.

ABSORPTION OF CHLORIDS BY AQUATIC PLANTS.

The considerable absorptive power of many aquatic plants for chlorids is interesting. The ash of *Nymphæa alba*, amounting to 7 to 10 per cent of the dry matter, was found to contain 9 to 23 per cent of chlorine and that of *Spirogyra nitida* 24 per cent. The ash of such plants does not always show a sufficient potassium content to bind all the chlorine present, hence a part of the latter will in such cases be present as sodium chlorid. In order to estimate the absorptive power of *Elodea canadensis*, the writer has determined the amount of chlorine in water which ran slowly through a basin in which this plant was cultivated, and found that besides some sulphate and calcium and magnesium bicarbonate the water contained, per liter, 4.5 mgr. chlorine, 1.6 mgr.

---

[1] Landw. Vers. Stat., 1869, p. 262.
[2] Revue Générale de Botanique, Vol. X, p. 177.

potassa, and 2.7 mgr. soda. On the determination of the amount of ash in the plant it was found to be 8.04 per cent, in which was 0.6 part chlorine, so that the plant therefore contained in the dry matter over one thousand times as much chlorine as an equal weight of the water in which it was grown.

SODIUM CHLORID IN ANIMALS.

Chlorine, in the form of sodium chlorid, plays an important rôle in animals, the formation of normal gastric juice being impossible in its absence. An idea of its great importance for the blood may be inferred from the fact that on an average about one-half of the blood ash consists of chlorid of sodium. Nearly one-third of the ash of the white of hens' eggs is made up of it. This salt can not be replaced by potassium chlorid, as the latter in the same quantity would exert a noxious influence on the animal. Generally, sodium salts exert an injurious effect on animals only when present in about five times larger quantities than potassium salts.

PHYSIOLOGICAL OCCURRENCE OF CALCIUM FLUORID.

The general occurrence of calcium fluorid in the teeth of animals renders very probable the supposition that it is present in many plants also, and indeed traces have been discovered in several cases. Fluorids, however, are not necessary for plants, the latter having been raised in culture solutions containing no trace of such compounds. It may be said that soluble fluorids in moderate amounts exert a poisonous action upon plants, as well as upon animals, and that they are more injurious to bacteria than to yeast—a fact of which practical use has been made in the manufacture of alcohol.

BEHAVIOR OF PLANTS TO POTASSIUM BROMID.

Bromine compounds occur normally in seaweeds, but as yet it is not known whether they are present in them only as organic or also as inorganic combinations. The physiological substitution of potassium bromid for potassium chlorid in the higher plants is impossible. In the case of buckwheat plants cultivated with potassium bromid, the writer observed that only one of six lived to bear a single seed, the others dying at or near the flowering stage; hence the recent assertion that bromids are not noxious for Phanerogams can be admitted only in the case of certain plants or a limited period of development.

RELATIONS OF ORGANISMS TO IODINE COMPOUNDS.

Since the discovery that an iodine compound occurs in the thyroid and the thymus glands of animals, it must inevitably be assumed that traces of iodine compounds must exist in soils and plants also. Gautier[1] has demonstrated that there are traces of iodine in the air of Paris.

[1] According to Gautier (1899), marine algæ contain in 100 grams dry matter 60 mgr. iodine, while fresh-water algæ contain only 0.25 to 2.40 mgr.

He determined also the amount of iodine in sea water to be 2.32 mgr. per liter.[1] Various marine organisms contain moderately large quantities of iodine. For instance, Harnack isolated iodospongin, containing on an average 8.2 per cent iodine, from marine sponges.

Drechsel[2] found in a protein, viz, the axial horny skeleton of the coral *Gorgonia cavolinii*, 7.7 per cent iodine. On decomposition with baryta this protein yields a compound of the composition of mono-iod-amido-butyric acid. Potassium or sodium iodid, even in small doses, exerts a poisonous influence on animals as well as on plants. Germinating buckwheat seeds placed in a full mineral solution in which the potassium was offered as iodid, died before the first leaf was developed, as the writer observed many years ago. The poisonous action of the iodid of potassium is no doubt due to the liberation of iodine by oxidation favored by the acid cell sap. Lower organisms without acid juices are rather indifferent in this respect. The writer found certain algæ and infusoria alive in culture water five weeks after 0.5 per cent of iodid of potassium had been added to it. On the other hand, 0.2 per cent potassium iodid killed larger kinds of *Spirogyra* within a few days when the culture solution contained traces of the acid monopotassium phosphate. Lower fungi and bacteria are not injured in neutral culture solutions to which even 1 per cent of this iodid is added. Potassium iodid has been found by bacteriologists to possess a germicidal action only when present in large doses.

THE PHYSIOLOGICAL RÔLE OF ALKALI SALTS.

IMPORTANCE OF POTASSIUM FOR THE FORMATION OF STARCH AND PROTEIN.

The paramount importance of potassium salts for every living cell is firmly established. In green plants they are concerned not only in the synthesis of carbohydrates, but also in that of the protein bodies, since not only is there an increase of potassium salts in such parts of green plants as are developing rapidly and consequently forming large amounts of protein, but most fungi, even in the presence of such a favorable nutrient as sugar, are found to require potassium salts for the production of protein. These salts can never be replaced by lithium[3] or sodium salts, but in certain fungi they may be replaced to a limited extent by rubidium or cæsium salts (p. 25).

It is a well-known fact that plants cultivated in the presence of more sodium than potassium salts will nevertheless absorb a greater quantity of the latter than of the former, and some plants grown on soil

---

[1] A part of this iodine is present in organisms and organic compounds.

[2] Zeitsch. f. Biologie, 1895, Vol. XV. Drechsel calls this protein "gorgonin." On decomposition it yielded not only iodine, but also 2 per cent chlorine (or bromine?).

[3] Although lithium salts exert a noxious action on Phanerogams they do not readily affect algæ. Spirogyra still appeared normal after four weeks in a complete culture solution to which 0.3 per mille lithium chlorid was added. At a higher concentration, however, the result may differ.

very rich in potassium salts will absorb almost no soda. The amount of potassa annually required per hectare of pine forest is about 7.5 kilos, of wheat field 37.5 kilos, of clover field 102 kilos, and of potato field 125 kilos. Other things being equal, an increase of potassa will increase to a certain degree the percentage of carbohydrates, and further, potassa is reported to be present in larger proportions in those parts in which the carbohydrates are transported, as in the parenchyma of the bark and pith.

Secondary potassium phosphate possibly forms loose combinations with proteins more easily than does sodium phosphate, since an increase of potassium phosphate is generally accompanied by an increase of proteins, as in the seeds. Pollen grains also seem to be rich in this salt; at least Ramann found that of the ash in the pine pollen 50.74 per cent was potassa and 30.08 per cent phosphoric acid. Seeds always contain much more potassium phosphate than sodium phosphate, while on the other hand the proportion of soda to potassa in form of other salts than phosphates is often found to be larger in the leaves and roots.[1]

The following table shows the composition of seeds of Gramineæ and Leguminosæ, the latter containing, as is known, relatively more protein than the former:

Analysis of the seeds of Gramineæ and Leguminosæ. *

Product analyzed.	Number of analyses.	Total ash. Average.	Average in 100 parts of ash.		Protein.
			Soda.	Potassa.	
		Per cent.	Per cent.	Per cent.	Per cent.
Gramineæ:					
Wheat	98	1.97	2.25	31.16	11.0
Rye	20	2.09	1.70	31.47	10.3
Barley.................................	50	2.60	2.53	20.15	10.1
Maize	9	1.51	1.83	27.93	10.0
Oats.................................	23	3.14	2.34	16.32	9.8
Millet	3	3.43	1.30	11.39	....
Average...........................	....	2.457	1.99	23.07	10.2
Leguminosæ:					
Vetch	3	3.10	7.86	30.14	27.9
Pea.................................	29	2.73	0.96	41.79	22.7
Lupin	3	3.95	0.37	29.84	35.3
Soy bean	1	2.83	1.08	47.00	33.2
Field bean (*Vicia*).	15	3.57	1.34	42.49	24.8
Garden bean (*Phaseolus*)................	13	3.22	1.49	44.01	24.3
Average...........................	....	3.23	2.17	39.21	29.0

* These figures were taken from E. Wolff's Aschen Analysen, Vol. I.

Calculating from the above data the amount of soda and potassa for 1,000 parts of dry organic matter, the seeds of Gramineæ contain 0.48 part soda and 5.67 parts potassa, while those of Leguminosæ contain 0.70 part soda and 12.66 parts potassa. It is seen, therefore, that there

[1] In some cases the amount of soda found in the leaves exceeds even that of potassa. Wolff's tables give for the leaf of *Daucus carota* a total ash content of 13.53 per cent for the dry matter, and for 100 parts of this ash 19.83 parts soda, but only 11.26 parts of potassa. The occasionally rather large soda content in the leaves is due to the current of transpiration, containing sodium salts among other things.

is more potassa in seeds which are richer in protein, but the proportions do not show any very close relation. For the Gramineæ the proportion of potassa to protein would be as 1 to 17, and for the Leguminosæ as 1 to 23. Hornberger's investigations[1] on the growth of maize showed the relation between potassa and protein nitrogen in the different periods of plant development to be for the leaves 1–1.1 to 1–1.8, or calculating from the protein itself, 1–6.8 to 1–12.2.

Although potassa is indispensable in the formation of carbohydrates, the quantitative proportions in the seeds show a closer relation to the protein than to the starch content of the seeds.[2]

BENEFICIAL ACTION OF SODIUM SALTS.

The fact that many kinds of plants have been raised to perfection in the absence of sodium salts proves that the latter have no indispensable function to perform in plant life. Stahl-Schroeder[3] recently inferred from his experiments what others also had already observed, that is, that sodium can not perform the special part of the functions of potassium which relates to the preparation of organic substances in plants. Nevertheless, sodium salts may sometimes exert a beneficial action, and several observers ascribe to them a promoting action in the ripening process of the Gramineæ. Wagner and Wolff have each reported favorably on the application of sodium salts, pointing out that as regards osmotic and neutralizing functions a replacement of potassium by sodium compounds is quite possible, which is of practical value, since the sodium salts are much cheaper than the potassium salts. In a recent article Dassonville[4] pointed out the beneficial action of sodium salts upon wheat. However, further control experiments along this line will be necessary.

CAN POTASSIUM SALTS BE REPLACED BY RUBIDIUM SALTS IN GREEN PLANTS AND IN ANIMALS?

Various authors have shown that potassium can not be replaced in plants by sodium or by lithium, starvation phenomena occurring with the former and toxical phenomena developing with the latter (Nobbe). As regards their atomic weight, sodium and lithium stand below while rubidium and cæsium stand above potassium, as follows:

$$
\begin{aligned}
&\left. \begin{aligned} Li &= 7 \\ Na &= 23 \end{aligned} \right\} \text{ diff.: } 16 \\
&K = 39 \quad \text{diff.: } 16 \\
&Rb = 85.4 \quad \text{diff.: } 16 \times 3 - 1.6 \\
&Ci = 133 \quad \text{diff.: } 16 \times 3 - 0.4
\end{aligned}
$$

---

[1] Landw. Jahrb., Vol. XI, p. 461.

[2] Fertilizing with potassium salts does not always increase the yield of grain. Frequently it is only the yield of straw that is increased. The form in which the potassium salts are given exerts much influence.

[3] Jour. f. Landw., Vol. XLVII, p. 78.

[4] Revue Générale de Botanique, 1898, Vol. X. He states also that "potassium silicate produces a dark green color."

Since the properties of elements are to a certain extent functions of their atomic weight, it might be supposed that the physiological capabilities of the alkali metals would increase with their atomic weight, but the facts observed are not in accord with this view. Birner and Lukanus[1] demonstrated that plants soon perish when the culture solutions contain rubidium or cæsium nitrate in place of potassium nitrate. In experiments with buckwheat plants the writer afterwards confirmed this conclusion as regards rubidium nitrate,[2] not taking cæsium salts into consideration; but he observed in addition that the action of rubidium chlorid differed to some extent from that caused by rubidium nitrate. Where the chlorid was offered the plants attained a greater height than with the nitrate. Those with rubidium nitrate died before the flowers were formed, while those with rubidium chlorid died after that period. Torsion and thickening of the stalk and curling and rolling up of the leaves were the most striking results with rubidium nitrate. In both cases, however, a diagnosis of the pathologic characters revealed essentially a disturbance in the functions of the chlorophyll bodies and in the transportation of starch, the effect on the latter being more marked with the nitrate than with the chlorid. A chemical comparison of buckwheat plants grown with potassium chlorid and of those grown with rubidium chlorid showed (1) that the ethereal extract of the "potassium plants" was of a normal pure green, while that of the "rubidium plants" was of a yellowish green; (2) that the rubidium plants contained 7.8 per cent of glucose in the dry matter, while the potassium plants contained none; (3) that there was more starch in the potassium plants than in the rubidium plants.

The writer has observed further that the replacement of even one-half of the potassium chlorid in a culture solution by rubidium chlorid will impede the development, the plants reaching after six weeks only half the size of the control plants. Moreover, the leaves were partially rolled in, the flowers were scanty, and the plants died before the seeds ripened.

These experiments proved that it is impossible to raise normal seed-bearing buckwheat plants when the chlorid of potassium in the culture solution is replaced by chlorid of rubidium, but on the other hand they left hardly any doubt that rubidium chlorid can serve for certain physiological functions of which sodium chlorid is utterly incapable. With rubidium chlorid, buckwheat plants may reach a dry weight of even thirty-three times that of the seeds,[3] but with sodium chlorid they seldom reach over five times. In a normally raised plant, however, the dry matter may be over six hundred times the weight of the seed. In the experiment with rubidium chlorid starch was formed by assimilation, but in those with sodium chlorid none was formed. The flowering stage was

[1] Landw. Vers. Stat., Vol. VII, p. 363.
[2] Ibid., Vol. XXI, p. 389.
[3] A certain writer's recent statement that rubidium salts have a poisonous effect on plants has to be somewhat modified.

reached[1] in the former case but not in the latter. With rubidium chlorid pathologic phenomena made their appearance chiefly after the flowering stage, but with sodium chlorid starvation phenomena were observed very much earlier.

Molisch had demonstrated that algæ can not develop if the potassium salts of the culture solution are replaced by rubidium salts.[2] In animals, also, neither cæsium nor rubidium salts can take the place of potassium salts, although a moderate amount of the rubidium salts is not noxious, and in large quantities they are even less injurious than the potassium salts.[3]

NECESSITY OF SODIUM SALTS FOR ANIMALS.

The great amount of sodium chlorid in the blood has already been mentioned, but the blood contains still other sodium salts of importance, such as sodium bicarbonate (in the ash of ox blood was found 14 to 18 per cent sodium carbonate) and the secondary sodium phosphate. Both these salts have an important bearing on the respiration process, as they carry in solution to the lungs for exhalation the carbonic acid produced by even the most remote cells of the body.

BEHAVIOR OF FUNGI TOWARD RUBIDIUM SALTS.

It has long been observed that mold fungi thrive in the presence of even very small quantities of potassium salts, traces of which are sometimes contained as impurities in certain organic compounds. These traces have to be considered in preparing culture solutions for special purposes. Yeast requires a larger amount of potassium, especially in the form of the primary and secondary phosphate, than do mold fungi. Certain kinds of microbes, such as *Anthrax* bacilli, do not develop well when the amount of potassium salts is very small. Sodium salts can not replace potassium salts even for these simple organisms, but rubidium salts can do so in certain cases, as in *Bacillus coli*, less successfully in *B. pyocyaneus*,[4] and still less in *Cladothrix*.[5] The writer has also established the fact that a mold fungus (*Penicillium*) and yeast can utilize rubidium and cæsium salts when the composition of the nourishing solution is otherwise very favorable and contains sugar and peptone. Günther's observation that the behavior of different mold fungi to rubidium salts varies, is interesting, these salts being utilized by *Botrytis cinerea*, but not by *Rhizopus nigricans*.[6] The less favorable

---

[1] It would be of considerable interest to investigate whether the buckwheat egg cell is properly fecundated when rubidium chlorid in place of potassium chlorid is offered.

[2] On the other hand no injurious influence upon algæ is noticed when to the complete culture solutions 0.3 per mille of the chlorids of rubidium or cæsium is added.

[3] According to Richet, the lethal minimum dose of rubidium in form of rubidium chlorid is 1 gram for 1 kilo body weight when applied subcutaneously. This is about twice as much as the lethal dose of potassium chlorid.

[4] Bot. Centralbl., 1898, No. 26.

[5] Winogradzki has shown that *Mycoderma vini* also can utilize rubidium salts to advantage, but not cæsium salts.

[6] Dissertation, Erlangen, 1897.

the organic nutrient is, however, the more will potassium show its superiority over rubidium. An observation which appears to throw some light on one physiological difference between potassium and rubidium salts may be mentioned here: The cultures of *Cladothrix* and of *Penicillium* formed floating masses in the solution containing potassium salts,[1] while they gradually sank to the bottom in those containing rubidium salts. As the swimming is probably caused by the presence of fatty matter, it seems that potassium salts are more favorable for producing fat than are rubidium salts. Further, spore formation is almost entirely prevented in *Penicillium* when rubidium is offered in place of potassium. Only after an increase of the magnesium sulphate was a scanty formation of spores noticed.

The secondary and primary phosphates are the most favorable forms in which to offer potassium salts to fungi. In case phosphoric acid is applied in combination with ammonia, potassium may be added as lactate or tartrate or as other assimilable organic salts.

Finally it may be mentioned that of all the alkali salts potassium salts exert the most powerful positive chemotaxis upon bacteria, and that next to them come rubidium salts (Pfeffer).

PHYSIOLOGICAL SUPERIORITY OF POTASSIUM SALTS.

The question as to what peculiar property of potassium its physiological capacity must be ascribed, implies also the questions: Why can the physiological functions of potassium salts not be performed by the related sodium salts? In reviewing all the properties of the two metals and of their compounds can not such chemical differences be discovered as would also explain the great physiological difference? Can there not be found in potassium chemical properties that give it a certain superiority over sodium? Long ago the writer searched for striking and characteristic differences and believes he is justified in calling attention to the following facts, which prove that potassium and its oxid can bring on in certain cases a so-called chemical condensation which sodium and its oxid can not. For instance, carbonic oxid can be condensed by potassium to triquinoyl, a benzene derivative, but not by sodium (Lerch, Nietzki). Phenol added to fusing potassium hydroxid, will, under condensation, yield diphenol among other things, but with sodium hydroxid, oxidation, but little condensation, is observed, resorcin and phloroglucin resulting (Barth).

Among other noticeable differences may be mentioned, (1) that certain potassium salts condense ethyl aldehyde to aldol, while sodium salts change it to croton aldehyde (Kopp and Michael); (2) that potas-

---

[1] The writer prepared the culture solutions with the purest materials, consisting in this case of—

	Per cent.
Sodium acetate	0.5
Glucose	1.0
Di-ammonium phosphate	.1
Magnesium sulphate	.02
Potassium tartrate	.10

sium acts on boiling triphenyl methane resulting in the development of hydrogen, but that sodium does not; (3) that potassium salicylate is converted at 210° C. into the isomeric paraoxybenzoate,[1] while in the sodium paraoxybenzoate just the reverse transformation is produced at 300° C. (Kolbe); (4) that potassium hydroxid decomposes peroxid of hydrogen more quickly than does sodium hydroxid (Schöne).

It seems very probable to the writer that from the physiological point of view the condensing properties of potassium are of prime importance. Substantial reasons exist for assuming chemical condensation processes, not only in the formation of carbohydrates and fat, but also in that of the proteins, i. e., in the three principal compounds of the plant cell. The writer called attention to this probable rôle of potassium salts in plants as early as 1880,[2] and still holds this explanation to be the correct one.

It is very probable that for the condensing operations the organoids of plant cells use a potassium protein compound. It is well known, of course, that chloroplasts require potassium salts for the assimilatory function and further that they have an alkaline reaction.[3] Finally, there can be no longer any doubt that sugars are produced by condensation.

As regards the formation of protein, the writer has on various occasions pointed out that certain facts, especially the great rapidity of protein formation in many instances and the absence of by-products and between-products, inevitably lead to the assumption that in this process also condensation plays an important part. But potassium salts are absolutely indispensable in animal life also, although the synthetical work performed is not so far-reaching as in plants. However, the formation of fat from sugar in the animal body requires condensation as well as reduction, while the formation of glycogen[4] from glucose and that of proteids from proteoses consists in dehydration and polymerization. In such cases potassium salts may play a rôle, and perhaps also in the processes of organization, as, for example, in the leucocytes and gland cells, which latter are in certain cases frequently renewed, or in the contractile substance of the muscles when work or starvation have destroyed a part of it.[5]

_____

[1] The corresponding rubidium salt in this case behaves similarly and therefore bears more resemblance to the potassium than to the sodium salt.

[2] Pflüger's Arch., Vol. XXII, p. 510.

[3] Molisch (Bot. Zeit., 1898, No. 2) observed that as soon as the cells are killed and the chloroplasts come in direct contact with the acid cell sap, the cells of _Coleus_ or _Perilla_, rich in chloroplasts and containing anthocyan in an acid cell sap, underwent the characteristic change from red to blue and green produced by alkaline liquids. Cells of the same plants which are poor in chloroplasts or free from them do not show this change.

[4] The liver, which is the principal organ in glycogen formation, contains, according to Oidtmann, three times more potassium than sodium, while in the spleen the proportion is, according to the same author, just the reverse.

[5] Organization, as it takes place in a developing organ, is one of the least-known vital processes. One thing, however, is sure, that is, that a connection of numerous protein molecules in groups of a higher order takes place. This connecting process was supposed by Pflüger to consist in polymerization or etherification.

Nägeli ascribed the differences in the physiological capacities of potassium and sodium salts to their different affinities for water. Sodium salts bind the water of crystallization, but corresponding potassium salts do not, and thus being free from such a dense sphere of water the latter are better qualified for katalytic work. The dense layer of water around the molecules of sodium salts would not only prevent the salt itself from coming into immediate contact with other molecules, but it also would impede an effectual transmission of vibrations. On this basis also Nägeli tries to explain the fact that the soil absorbs potassium salts better than it does sodium salts, claiming that the latter are prevented by their water mantle from following the attracting forces.[1] However, objections can be easily raised against this view, the most serious one being that by no means has every sodium salt the water of crystallization.

THE PHYSIOLOGICAL RÔLE OF CALCIUM AND MAGNESIUM SALTS.

DISTRIBUTION OF LIME AND MAGNESIA IN PLANTS.

It has long been known that calcium and magnesium salts can not physiologically replace each other, and the question as to the functions of these salts has until recently been a matter of conjecture. The striking regularity with which the leaves of plants show a relative increase in lime, while the seeds show an increase in magnesia, has furnished a clue to the mystery of the action of these salts. A number of cases will serve to illustrate that different parts of the same plant contain quite different proportions of lime and magnesia. Let us first consider the leaves of the Gramineæ, since in them the absence of calcium oxalate excludes a misleading factor. The following data are taken from tables in Liebig's work:[2]

Per cents of lime and magnesia in the ash of the grain and the straw of Gramineæ.

	Magnesia.	Lime.
Grains of—		
Barley	8.29	2.48
Oats	7.70	3.70
Wheat	11.75	3.30
Maize	13.60	0.57
Rye (bran)	15.82	3.47
Straw of—		
Barley	2.97	7.28
Oats	4.58	7.29
Wheat	1.69	6.93
Maize	1.84	5.33
Rye	2.41	9.06

A better basis for a comparative estimate will be obtained if the average of these figures is taken and compared with the relative number of molecules instead of the absolute weight. The seeds of Gramineæ will

---

[1] Sitzungsber. d. Bayr. Akad. Wiss, 1879, p. 348.

[2] Die Chemie in ihrer Anwendung auf Agrikultur und Physiologie, 7 ed., Part I. The analyses were made by Way and Ogsten, Weber, and others.

then be found to contain for every 17 molecules of lime 100 molecules of magnesia, while in the straw there will be found fully 224 molecules of lime for every 100 molecules of magnesia. The leaves of *Phaseolus vulgaris* contain in comparison to the magnesia content four times as much lime as the seeds, and those of *Brassica napus* seven times as much. The proportion of magnesia to lime in tobacco leaves was found to be, on an average, as 1 to 5. The proportion of these constituents in the flowers is also different from that in the leaves. For example, in the case of *Humulus lupulus* there was found in the—

Flowers...1 part magnesia to 2 parts lime.
Leaves...1 part magnesia to 6 parts lime.

On comparing the underground parts of the plants with the leaves, it was also found that the latter contain more lime. For example, it was observed in—

Daucus carota, roots ....1 part magnesia to 2. 5 parts lime.
leaves.............................1 part magnesia to 14. 0 parts lime.
Solanum tuberosum, tubers.......................1 part magnesia to . 6 part lime.
leaves ....1 part magnesia to 6. 1 parts lime.

Very great differences are revealed also in the comparison of the wood with the seeds in this regard, the lime content being relatively increased in the wood:

Abies pectinata, seeds.............................1 part magnesia to 0. 09 part lime.
wood ....1 part magnesia to 4. 62 parts lime.
Pinus sylvestris, seeds.............................1 part magnesia to . 12 part lime.
wood ....1 part magnesia to 1. 60 parts lime.

For the fruiting year of a beech tree 150 years old, R. Weber[1] several years ago made some interesting observations on the migration of magnesia. He found that magnesia as well as nitrogen migrates from the trunk to the points of seed formation, and in a smaller measure also sulphuric and phosphoric acids do the same. The decrease of the magnesia in the wood extended to ninety annual rings. The wood of the tree was analyzed in zones of thirty rings each. The percentage of lime and magnesia in the ash are given as follows, as is also for comparison the composition of a beech tree of the same age which had grown near by, but which bore no fruits that year:

Lime and magnesia in a fruiting beech and in a control beech.

Part of tree.	Beech tree in fruit. In the ash—		Beech tree not in fruit. In the ash—	
	Lime.	Magnesia.	Lime.	Magnesia.
	Per cent.	*Per cent.*	*Per cent.*	*Per cent.*
Bark	85. 05	2. 60	82. 10	3. 65
Zone 1..	33. 92	12. 65	27. 69	29. 25
Zone 2..	34. 13	11. 95	31. 52	26. 72
Zone 3..	35. 98	12. 15	33. 55	20. 39
Zone 4..	33. 36	13. 36	27. 59	19. 02
Zone 5 (heartwood)	....	....	31. 21	11. 00

[1] Forstl. Naturw. Zeitschr., 1892.

As shown by the table, there was relatively a most striking decrease of magnesia to lime in zones 1, 2, and 3 of the trunk of the seed beech as compared with the corresponding zones from the control beech.

The leaves of aquatic plants are also rich in lime. The proportions of magnesia and lime were found to be, in *Nymphœa lutea*, 1:8.5; in *Lemna*, 1:3.3 to 1:7.6; and in *Elodea canadensis*, 1:8.4. Also algæ show similar proportions, as seen from the ash analyses of *Spirogyra nitida* by Pennington (1896) and of fucoids by Gödschens (1854). Algæ incrustated with calcium carbonate must, of course, be here excluded.

From what has been said under this head it will be seen that the analytical investigations of the ash of plants show (1) that lime and magnesia are present in every part of the plant, and (2) that the leaves contain relatively more lime and the seeds relatively more magnesia than the other parts of the plants. These characteristics can not be accidental, but must be the result of certain functions.

THE PHYSIOLOGICAL IMPORTANCE OF LIME SALTS IN PLANTS.

The more leaf surface is developed in a given time, the more lime is necessary. A normal crop of wheat requires per hectare (nearly 2.5 acres) about 11.6 kilos; sugar beets, 30.2 kilos; grass, 49.4 kilos; clover, 111.8 kilos; and tobacco, 153.7 kilos, while a normal growth of wood needs annually about 20 kilos of lime, besides 7 to 16 kilos of magnesia, 2 to 10 kilos of potash, and 0.8 to 4 kilos of phosphoric acid. When the large demand for lime salts by plants is taken into consideration, it is easily understood that an absence or deficiency of lime becomes apparent very early.

Stohmann[1] kept maize shoots alive for some time in a culture solution free from lime, but all development gradually ceased with the consumption of the stored-up lime. However, when at the end of several weeks some calcium nitrate was added, a very striking effect was noticed, hardly five hours elapsing before new buds pushed out from the sickly looking tips.

Heiden[2] observed that maize and peas in culture solutions without lime lived only four weeks, and reached respectively only 18.9 and 27 cm. in height. In culture solutions without magnesia, however, maize lived ten to twelve weeks and peas lived eight weeks and attained a height of 44 and 30 cm. respectively. In solutions without potassa or phosphoric acid, but otherwise complete, such plants lived from eight to twelve weeks. The absence of lime, therefore, was felt first, owing

---

[1] Ann. Chem. Pharm., Vol. CXXI.

[2] Centralbl. f. Agr. Chem., Vol. XVII, p. 622. Prianishnikow observed that shoots develop quicker in a solution of gypsum than in distilled water, which fully accords with the writer's observations. Seedlings of *Phaseolus*, *Pisum*, and *Cucurbita* kept in distilled water die before all the reserve material is consumed. An addition of a calcium salt to the distilled water leads, however, to the perfect exhaustion of the reserve stores (Boehm, Liebenberg).

probably to the relatively small amount of lime in the reserve store of the seeds.

Palladin[1] placed etiolated leaves of *Vicia faba* on the surface of distilled water, on a 10 per cent cane-sugar solution, and on solutions of 0.3 per cent calcium nitrate with and without the addition of cane sugar, but a noticeable growth was observed only where both sugar and calcium nitrate were present. The same author[2] has found that etiolated leaves of *Vicia faba* contain less lime than do green leaves. His analysis showed that there were contained in 1,000 parts of green leaves 13.3 parts of lime, but in 1,000 parts of etiolated leaves only 2.6 parts of lime. The former yielded 10.3 per cent of ash, the latter 7.54 per cent. Stoklasa found in diseased leaves of the sugar beet less than half the amount of lime present in healthy leaves of this plant.

Church's investigations[3] with albino leaves demonstrated that the composition of their ash is very different from the ash of healthy leaves, as the potassa is considerably increased in the white leaves, while on the contrary the lime is more abundant in the green leaves. It is to be regretted, however, that the author did not determine separately the amount of lime present as oxalate and as carbonate and that portion of the lime belonging to the organized matter itself, calculating the results for equal surfaces in both cases. It is also very characteristic that the lime content of the phanerogamic parasite Cuscuta, which forms no chloroplasts in the full-grown state, amounts to only 2 per cent in the ash, while the clover, its host, is very rich in lime.

Another interesting case, showing a decrease in lime content in diseased leaves, was observed by Dr. Erwin F. Smith in his studies of the peach yellows. He gives the percentage of lime in the ash of the healthy leaves, according to analyses made by Mr. N. E. Knorr, as 40.58, and in the diseased leaves as only 23.88.[4] According to a later analysis, made by Dr. Eastwood at Dr. Smith's request, the ash content of healthy twigs of one season's growth is given as 2.10 to 2.58 per cent and that of diseased twigs as only 1.6 per cent, and of healthy twigs from another orchard as 1.4 per cent and of diseased twigs as only 1 per cent.[5] In these cases the amount of lime was also less in the diseased

[1] Ber. d. Deut. Bot. Ges., 1891, p. 230.

[2] Ibid, Vol. X, p. 179.

[3] Jour. Chem. Soc., 1878 and 1886. The investigations were made with *Quercus rubra* bearing some albino branches, and also with albino leaves of *Plectogyne variegata* and of *Hedera helix.*

[4] Smith, Erwin F., Bull. No. 4, Division of Botany, U. S. Dept. of Agr.

[5] Smith, Erwin F., Bull. No. 4, Division of Vegetable Physiology and Pathology, U. S. Dept. of Agr.

leaves, while potassa, magnesia, and in most cases phosphoric acid also were relatively increased, as will be seen from the following table:

Analytical data from diseased and healthy trees from four orchards.

[Per cents in the ash.]

	Orchard A, at Magnolia, Del.		Orchard B, at Dover, Del.		Orchard C, at Magnolia, Del.		Orchard D, at Still Pond, Md.	
	Healthy.	Dis-eased.	Healthy.	Dis-eased.	Healthy.	Dis-eased.	Healthy.	Dis-eased.
Calcium oxid	40.58	23.88	61.21	47.61	48.85	43.68	40.54	34.75
Magnesium oxid	4.81	5.97	5.62	7.65	3.21	4.31	2.85	10.23
Potassium oxid	15.52	31.86	15.02	20.19	28.26	32.51	30.18	30.76
Phosphoric acid	7.55	13.79	10.63	12.63	10.45	9.29	12.00	16.86

The observations which Honda and the writer[1] made with young pine trees cultivated in pure quartz sand moistened with culture solutions free from lime have shown that the leaves reached only half their normal size, and that the young trees gradually perished.

Bokorny[2] has cultivated algæ (*Spirogyra, Zygnema,* and *Mesocarpus*) in culture solutions, in one of which there was no lime, in another no magnesia, and in a third neither lime nor magnesia. These culture solutions were kept in aluminium vessels to avoid any trace of substances derived from glass. In the complete solution a normal formation in every respect was noticed. In the solution in which lime was absent the first phenomenon to occur was a decrease of chlorophyll, the chlorophyll band of *Spirogyra* diminishing not only in breadth and thickness, but also in length, and the original spiral finally becoming a straight line parallel to the longer axis. Some starch, however, was still produced, which proves that it is not the lack of organic matter and of potassa which here brings on this shrinkage, and that the result can be attributed only to the absence of lime. In the solutions in which magnesia and lime magnesia alone were absent, the volume of the nucleus decreased considerably, as well as that of the chlorophyll bodies. The writer has repeatedly observed that *Spirogyra majuscula* collected from swamps containing only traces of lime had very slender chlorophyll bands and scarcely any starch, but that they contained much stored-up albumin. When placed in culture solutions containing a moderate amount of lime salts the bands soon became broader.

Rudolph Weber[3] instituted a series of experiments with cultures of peas under glass of different colors, and compared these plants with

---

[1] Coll. of Agr., Bull., Vol. II, No. 6, Tokyo, Japan.

[2] Bot. Centralbl., 1895, No. 14. The complete solution contained—

	Per cent.
Potassium nitrate	0.04
Potassium sulphate	.03
Monopotassium phosphate	.03
Calcium nitrate	.03
Magnesium sulphate	.03

[3] Landw. Vers. Stat., 1875, Vol. XVIII, p. 19.

plants grown in very faint light and with normal control plants. The plants were grown in purified quartz sand and watered with culture solutions in equal quantities. The culture was terminated after forty-four days, because the plants under violet and green glass began at that time to show signs of approaching death. The analyses of the ash gave some interesting results, especially as regards the lime content, and are as follows:

Comparative amounts of magnesia, lime, and potassa per thousand parts of dry matter of normal and etiolated plants and plants grown under different colored glass.

Condition of plant.	Magnesia.	Lime.	Potassa.
	Per cent.	*Per cent.*	*Per cent.*
Normal	10.2	32.1	48.5
Etiolated	6.7	12.4	44.9
Under green glass	8.3	13.2	56.5
Under violet glass	8.5	20.2	45.6
Under red glass	9.5	24.3	56.5
Under blue glass	8.8	30.2	61.1
Under yellow glass	9.5	30.3	53.2

The amount of phosphoric acid varied only from 16.7 to 20.5 per cent. The etiolated plants and those under green glass contained the smallest amount of lime, and a certain relation of the lime content to assimilation or rather to the plastids is evident.

VIEWS ON THE FUNCTIONS OF LIME SALTS.

Boehm[1] observed irregularities in the transportation of starch when lime salts were absent in the culture solutions. The plants (*Phaseolus multiflorus*) recovered[2] on the addition of calcium salts, while on the other hand the addition of magnesium salts hastened their death. The irregularity of behavior in the absence of lime consisted in the accumulation of starch in the pith and bark of the lower part of the stem. The death of the affected plants commenced generally in the upper parts of the stems and gradually spread to the lower parts. Boehm further attributed to the lime a function in the formation of the cell wall. He says: "In order to form the cell wall from starch and sugar, lime is just as important as for the formation of the bone. The lime forms the skeleton of the cell wall." One author,[3] however, claims that Boehm's inferences are not justified, as he had studied only one case. Some authors have even gone so far as to assert that lime salts are by no means required for every part of a plant, and one author concluded that leaves of *Tradescantia* may be raised without lime, another that the young wood is free of lime, and a third that *Fucus* may be found with-

---

[1] Ber. Akad. d. Wissensch., Wien, 1875.

[2] The addition of calcium chlorid, however, did not prevent death, probably owing to the liberation of hydrochloric acid when the attempt is made by the plant to assimilate the lime from this salt.

[3] Liebenberg, Ber. Akad. d. Wiss., Wien, 1881.

out a trace of lime.[1] These statements, however, were based principally on microscopical tests and could not be upheld. Some new leaves of *Tradescantia* may indeed develop completely when the branches are kept in distilled water, since, as the writer has observed, the nodes contain a considerable amount of stored-up lime. As to the assertion in regard to young wood, Weber's analyses[2] have revealed a considerable amount of lime in its ash. For example, 1 cubic meter (Festmeter) of the wood of *Larix* was found to contain 700 grams of lime, of which 112.4 grams belonged to the young wood. The young wood of *Fagus* contained about 29 per cent of lime in the ash. As regards the *Fucus* referred to above, it was only its cell sap that proved to be free from lime, while an examination of the organized parts revealed lime in them.

Thus far the only plants which have been proved positively to develop without lime salts are lower forms of algæ and fungi (p. 44).

Like Boehm, Schimper observed an abnormal accumulation of starch where there was a deficiency of lime. but he declares this to be a mere secondary pathological phenomenon, and pointed out that even leaves which are packed with starch may die. This, however, can not be regarded as a refutation of Boehm's views. In order to render starch available for respiration it must be saccharified. In Schimper's case a failure to produce diastase might adequately account for the result. Other discrepancies between the observations of several authors may have their origin in the different lime content of the seeds used for the experiment.

Raumer[3] agrees with Boehm in ascribing to the lime the function of aiding in the growth and solidification of the cell walls, but he does not agree with his other views. However, his reason for believing that lime has nothing to do with the transportation of starch is not convincing Certainly, the mere chemical process of forming starch from sugar does not require lime, but the production of the plastids—the indispensable apparatus for starch formation—may require it.

Holzner's view[4] that lime salts aid in the assimilation of sulphuric and phosphoric acids is very improbable, since his hypothesis would require the formation of oxalic acid in every protein-producing cell—a condition which is not realized; and, moreover, the assimilation of these acids also takes place in fungi in the absence of every trace of lime salts. Finally, Hornberger[5] and others have objected to this view as not agreeing with their observations.

---

[1] Boehm's hypothesis was entirely misconstrued by one author, who believed he had refuted it by showing that the migrating sugar is not bound to lime—a fact that might have been foreseen, as such a compound would be decomposed quickly by carbonic acid.

[2] Forstlich. Naturw. Zeitschr., 1892, p. 6, and 1893, p. 215.

[3] Landwirtsch. Vers. Stat., 1883, Vol. XXIX, p. 271.

[4] Flora, 1867, p. 497.

[5] Landw. Jahrb., 1882, Vol. XI, p. 455.

The functions of lime salts are believed by Schimper and others to consist in merely effecting certain processes of metabolism. Schimper[1] found that in the absence of lime the acid potassium oxalate accumulates in the leaves and buds and acts as a poison, hence calcium salts are useful, inasmuch as they precipitate the oxalic acid and thus prevent its noxious action. P. Groom[2] suggested that the injurious action of the acid potassium oxalate consists in retarding the action of diastase on starch, and thus its presence in the assimilating tissue brings about an accumulation of starch, due to the arrest of its transformation into sugar; then, as the soluble oxalate accumulates, there is also a retardation in the formation of starch, and this finally leads to the death of the protoplasm. Groom's theory, however, does not explain why calcium is required by plants also that do not form oxalic acid, hence the bad effects caused by a deficiency of lime must be explained in some other way. Although *Equisetaceæ* and most ferns and grasses, and even some species of the *Solanaceæ* and *Liliaceæ* are free from calcium oxalate, they all nevertheless require lime.

Neither Schimper nor Groom have raised the question as to why oxalates, even if neutral, exert a poisonous action on chlorophyll-bearing plants, while to the writer this question appeared to be the most important in this connection.

The greater lime content of the green parts first led the writer to suppose that the chlorophyll bodies might contain calcium compounds, and on the basis of this hypothesis he inaugurated a series of investigations. Among other things, these showed that the neutral oxalates are not poisonous to the lower fungi and that the development of these is not at all retarded by adding considerable quantities of neutral potassium oxalate to the culture solutions. Beer yeast is not injured by adding even as much as 4 per cent of this salt to a fermenting mixture. As in such cases the lime would become insoluble and its assimilation would thus be frustrated, the writer has come to the conclusion that these organisms do not require lime.[3] This is different in the case of the higher algæ, however. As the chlorophyll bodies of *Spirogyra* possess a highly differentiated structure, and even slight evil effects readily manifest themselves in certain changes along their margin, in the retraction of the lobes, etc., vacuolation of the chloroplasts, this alga was selected for the test. When *Spirogyra majuscula* was put into a 2 per cent solution of neutral potassium oxalate, a very striking fact was brought out, many of the chlorophyll bands being injured in even as short a time as thirty to forty minutes, while in even less time the nucleus showed a remarkable contraction, dwindling to a mere thread and thus causing a constriction of the cytoplasm where the plasma

---

[1] Flora, 1890, p. 209.

[2] Bot. Centralbl., 1896, No. 33.

[3] Erroneous representations in regard to this point have been refuted by the writer in Bot. Centralbl., 1898, Vol. LXXIV.

strings were attached. Moreover, filaments of *Spirogyra* which had been exposed for only ten minutes to the action of this oxalate solution and had still preserved their full turgor, were incapable of repairing the injury done after returning them to well water rich in lime, and they died after twenty-four hours. Even five minutes' action ultimately caused death. In a weaker solution (0.5 per cent) of oxalate the nucleus does not shrink to a thread, but slowly swells up and finally becomes an irregular, scalloped figure. In a still higher dilution (0.1 per cent) the poisonous action proceeds so slowly that it requires a number of days to completely kill all the cells.

In other species of algæ, such as *Vaucheria, Mougeotia, Zygnema, Cosmarium, Œdogonium, Chladophora, Sphæroplea*, etc, death, accompanied by swelling of the chlorophyll bodies, occurred after twenty-four hours' action of a solution of 0.5 per cent. Diatoms died in this solution in fifteen hours, but in a solution of 0.05 per cent some diatoms were still alive after three days. In higher dilutions the poisonous properties decrease rapidly.[1] Phanerogams also are easily attacked by oxalates. When placed in a 2 per cent solution of neutral potassium oxalate, the nucleus of an onion shows a contraction of about one-fifth of its normal diameter within ten to fifteen minutes. Leaves of *Elodea canadensis* and *Vallisneria spiralis* were killed completely in thirty-six hours[2] in a 1 per cent solution. The control experiments with potassium tartrate or sulphate, failed in all cases to show similar action. The claim, therefore, that lime salts are necessary to precipitate tartaric acid in plants that contain tartrates instead of oxalates has no support, since neutral tartrates are not poisonous, as are neutral oxalates.

The cytoplasm succumbs last, and its death is probably a secondary effect, due to the death of the nucleus and the chlorophyll body. Indeed it can be easily seen that the cytoplasm dies sooner when the number of chlorophyll bodies contained in it is increased. It is on this account that the circulation of the cytoplasm lasts much longer in the root hairs of *Chara* when under the influence of a dilute solution (0.5 per cent) of potassium oxalate than it does in the cells of the internodes filled with chlorophyll bodies. An equally dilute solution of neutral potassium tartrate shows no injurious action in the same length of time. The writer's explanation of the poisonous action is as follows: Judging from the most characteristic properties of soluble oxalates, that of precipitating lime from even highly diluted solutions of lime salts and that of depriving lime compounds generally of their lime and of converting it into the insoluble oxalate, he inferred from the peculiar poisonous action the existence of calcium protein compounds in the organized particles from which the nucleus and

[1] This, however, is not the case with free oxalic acid (p. 38).

[2] There are some remarkable cases in which monopotassium oxalate exists in the cell sap and still produces no injury, as, for instance, in *Rumex* and *Oxalis*. In these cases it is necessary to assume an unusual density of the tonoplasts—that is, a density sufficient to protect the nucleus and protoplasm.

the chlorophyll bodies are built up. Such organized calcium compounds would have a well-defined capacity for imbibition, which would change with the replacement of the calcium by another metallic element, and this altered water content must lead to a disturbance in the structure, which must prove fatal if not remedied in its initial stages. A peculiarity of protoplasm is that alteration of the structure is soon followed by the chemical change from the active to the passive modification of its proteids. Now, when potassium oxalate acts on the inferred calcium protein compounds they yield in addition to calcium oxalate the corresponding potassium protein compounds, which, on account of the different capacity for imbibition, can not physiologically replace the calcium compound. Moreover, neither tartr.te nor sulphate (which act much less energetically than the oxalate on calcium compounds[1]) attack the nucleus or the chlorophyll bodies. This also shows plainly that it is impossible to accept the view that potassium oxalate becomes dissociated in the cells and that it is the free oxalic acid which, on account of its acidity, kills the nucleus, since potassium nitrate would be expected to act in just the same way.[2]

It will of course be difficult to prove microchemically the formation of calcium oxalate in the chlorophyll body or nucleus when potassium oxalate is left to act upon them, since the amount of calcium in them is naturally very small, judging from the great molecular weight of the organized proteids with which it would be combined. Moreover the formation of distinct crystals of calcium oxalate would be impeded by the peculiar consistency of the living structures. It was claimed that in view of the highly complicated conditions in the cells the assumption of a direct connection between a working cause and an observed pathological result could not be admitted, as the latter might be simply the effect of primarily produced "disturbances of nutrition." However, this claim can not be sustained in the case of the action of neutral oxalates upon the nuclei, for in the first place this proceeds very rapidly in concentrations of over 1 per cent, and in the second place the processes of metabolism in objects like *Spirogyra* proceed very slowly.

Further observations by Migula[3] deserve to be mentioned here, as they demonstrate that free oxalic acid is among the most poisonous of organic acids. For example, in a solution of 0.004 per cent of free

---

[1] Calcium tartrate dissolves in about 2,000 parts of water.

[2] When acting on *Spirogyra* the potassium oxalate seems to pass direct to the nucleus through the plasma strings and not through the tonoplast, but on the other hand when potassium oxalate is contained in the cell sap of certain plants it seems to be confined there by the density of the tonoplast, which also prevents its direct contact with the nucleus in this case. In this connection Migula observed some interesting facts with *Spirogyra* kept in well water to which very small quantities of organic acids had been added. These were gradually oxidized in the cells into oxalic acid of which some was retained as neutral oxalate in the cell sap, and yielded a precipitate of calcium oxalate when placed in a diluted solution of lime salts.

[3] The Influence of Dilute Acids on Algæ (Breslau, 1888).

oxalic acid the nucleus of *Spirogyra orbicularis* was observed to swell up, frequently to six times its normal volume, and become turbid and opaque, while the cytoplasm still remained alive for some time. In concentrated solutions the cells die too quickly to show such character- istic symptoms, their death being due chiefly in this case to mere acidity.

When some filaments of *Spirogyra majuscula* were placed in 500 cc. of a solution of free oxalic acid[1] in even as high dilution as 0.0001 per cent, the writer observed great injury to some of the threads after five days. In most of the cells the plasma strings were retracted, the nucleus was contracted and rolled to the cell wall, and the sinuate margins of the chlorophyll bands were swollen up and numerous little drops became visible in them.[2] A very striking feature was the long-continued per- sistence of the turgor under these conditions, this being due to the cytoplasm remaining alive for a considerable time. In equally diluted solutions of tartaric acid most of the cells were perfectly normal after nine days, which shows that the character of acidity at this high dilu- tion exerted merely a secondary influence, and that this alone can not account for the action of the highly diluted oxalic acid.

FORMATION OF LIME INCRUSTATIONS.

It may not be out of place here to say a few words about the forma- tion of incrustations of calcium carbonate on certain aquatic plants, especially *Chara*—a phenomenon which Pringsheim[3] tries to explain on the hypothesis that by assimilation of the dissolved carbonic acid the neutral calcium carbonate is produced from the bicarbonate. However, the fact that not every plant growing in the same water and near *Chara* shows the incrustation must lead to the assumption that either the assimilation is of much greater energy in *Chara* than in many other plants, or that the surface of this plant is especially adapted for the absorption of the neutral calcium carbonate.

Hassack[4] advanced another hypothesis, that is, that the plants secrete an alkaline carbonate, which decomposes the calcium bicarbon- ate. However, the writer has proved this view to be entirely erro- neous.[5] The reaction with phenol phthalein, which Hassack used is not due to an alkaline carbonate, but to neutral calcium carbonate in a colloidal condition. Even the warming of ordinary water rich in calcium carbonate will produce ephemerally a red color with phenol- phthalein.

[1] Purest water distilled from glass vessels was used for all experiments with *Spirogyra*.

[2] Considerable swelling of the nucleus took place in a solution of 0.01 per cent oxalic acid.

[3] Jahrb. f. Wiss. Bot., Vol. XIX, p. 138.

[4] Unters. aus d. Bot. Instit. Tübingen, Vol. II, pp. 469–475.

[5] Flora, 1893, No. 4.

CAN CALCIUM IN PLANT CELLS BE REPLACED BY STRONTIUM?

It has long been recognized that calcium salts can not be replaced by potassium salts or sodium salts. Were it a well-founded hypothesis that calcium salts serve only for certain phases of metabolism and are not connected with more important properties of the protoplasm itself, then there might be taken a plain chemical view of the matter, that is, that the action of the bivalent elements is often different from that of the monovalent elements. Thus, for example, dextrose yields saccharin[1] when treated with lime, but not when treated with potassa (Kiliani); calcium carbamate yields calcium cyanamide upon heating, while potassium carbamate yields potassium cyanate (Drechsel); barium dibromsuccinate yields monobrommaleic acid on boiling of the aqueous solution, while the sodium salt yields monobrommalic acid.

It is certainly not the bivalent character of calcium, however, that determines its physiological value, for in that case barium or strontium might fulfill the same office, which is impossible. The inability of barium to do this might be explained by the most characteristic property of soluble barium salts, which is to precipitate sulphuric acid from even high dilution of sulphates, hence in plants the assimilation of sulphur from sulphates would become an impossibility. However, it would still be difficult to explain why barium salts are poisonous for animals, and also why strontium salts can not replace calcium salts in either plants or animals.[2]

The more intimate the connection between the functions of the lime and the vital properties of the cells, the more difficulty will naturally be encountered in an endeavor to substitute strontium for calcium, and experiments made in this connection argue against the possibility of the substitution. The writer made some experiments with an alga (*Spirogyra*) in 1892 which demonstrated that although this alga can remain healthy for several weeks at the ordinary temperature in a culture solution containing strontium nitrate in place of calcium nitrate, its further growth is nevertheless impeded, and moreover, that there is soon a noxious influence at a higher temperature (28° C.). Thus, for example, many cells died when kept at 28° C. in a solution of 0.3 per cent strontium nitrate, but this was not the case in a 0.3 per cent solution of calcium nitrate. This conclusion has been essentially confirmed by Molisch, who observed the interesting fact that the cell plate in the process of cell division is not properly formed when strontium salts are present in place of calcium salts. This occurs even when a small amount of a calcium salt is present, in which case the injurious effects of the strontium salt are not entirely prevented. The cell plate is the result of the work of the nuclear spindle, and the supposition that the cause of this defective work is attributable to a diseased condition of the nucleus seems justifiable. If the lime were not concerned in the

---

[1] This product is not the sweet saccharin of commerce.
[2] Only certain enzym actions form exceptions, as Bertrand has shown for pectase.

most intimate working of the nucleus the phenomenon in question would hardly be intelligible.

Similar experiments with beans and maize were inaugurated later on by Haselhoff,[1] but he offered calcium and strontium salts together in the beginning and gradually diminished the lime in the culture solution. The plants, however, very probably made use of the occasion to store up a certain amount of lime, which they may have used in the later period, and hence his conclusion that a substitution of calcium for strontium salts is possible can not be admitted.

The writer made an experiment with a phanerogamous plant also. Branches of *Tradescantia*, from 12.5 to 12.8 cm. long, were placed in solutions of—

	Per cent.
(1) Calcium nitrate	0.2
(2) Strontium nitrate	.2
(3) Calcium and strontium nitrate, each	.1

At a temperature of 10–15° C. a decided difference was noticed after twelve days. In the calcium nitrate solution young rootlets 0.5 cm. in length had appeared, but in the strontium nitrate solution only minute knobs were visible. Gradually a difference was also evident between the calcium nitrate and the calcium and strontium nitrate solutions. the root hairs in the former being long and numerous, while in the latter they were short and few. However. when the strontium nitrate gradually attained an excess over the calcium salts stored up in the branches, the noxious effect became evident, they having attained a length after forty-two days of only 13 and 13.3 cm., with only two or three leaves on each branch, while those in the solution of calcium nitrate attained a length of 16, 17.2, and 18 cm., with six to seven leaves on each branch. The leaves of the former branches were partially dying, but those of the latter were still healthy. A control case with distilled water demonstrated beyond a doubt that in the case of the strontium nitrate solution the phenomena mentioned were not merely due to the absence of the lime, but to a direct noxious action of the strontium salts. The numerous root hairs which developed in the distilled water further justified the conclusion that lime salts were stored up in the stems. Indeed the writer has demonstrated that besides sulphates. the nodes of the *Tradescantia* stems have stored up in them nitrates. potassium, and magnesium and calcium salts. An undeniable analogy appears to exist, therefore, between the noxious effect of the strontium salts and that of magnesium salts (p. 42), both beginning to be noxious when the amount of lime falls below a certain limit.

A series of very instructive experiments were recently carried out by U. Susuki[2] with five phanerogamous plants—*Hordeum, Fagopyrum esculentum, Phlox paniculata, Rubus idœus,* and *Coreopsis tinctoria.* Some of the plants were watered with a normal solution containing calcium in the form of calcium nitrate and others with solutions in which the calcium nitrate was replaced by equivalent quantities of strontium nitrate and of barium nitrate. Only the plants in the normal solutions showed a strong and vigorous development, while those in the barium and strontium solutions exhibited gradually an injurious action, and when at the time of their early death the experiment was terminated, the following data were obtained:

Action of calcium, strontium, and barium salts.

BUCKWHEAT SHOOTS.

	Nitrate of calcium.	Nitrate of strontium.	Nitrate of barium.
Average weight of one stem	0.352	0.260	0.187
Average weight of one leaf	.198	.080	.050

BARLEY SHOOTS.

	Nitrate of calcium.	Nitrate of strontium.	Nitrate of barium.
Average weight of one plant	1.50	0.67	0.51
Ratio of dry weight	100.00	44.06	34.00

It will be noticed that the action of the barium solution was more injurious than that of the strontium solution. Branches of the other three Phanerogams mentioned were used, here those in the barium and strontium solution died after eight days, while those in the normal solution containing calcium nitrate remained healthy and developed new leaves. Control cases in distilled water showed here also that the injury in the case of the barium solution is due not merely to the absence of lime, but directly to a poisonous influence of the barium and strontium salts. Further tests showed that these poisonous actions are retarded by the addition of lime salts.

Now, if calcium salts act only in processes of metabolism it might be inferred that such processes could be performed as well by strontium salts, the main properties of the salts of both elements being to a certain degree alike. Thus, strontium oxalate dissolves with difficulty in water (1:12,000), as does also the sulphate. The latter, however, being less soluble (1:6,895) than calcium sulphate (1:488), it might be supposed that the assimilation of sulphur is seriously lessened. However, considering the diluted state in which the phosphates enter and still how well they are assimilated, it is clear that the lesser degree of solubility of strontium sulphate would not be a serious obstacle to the assimilation of sulphur. It may then well be asked what kinds of processes of metabolism in plants have to be assumed for calcium salts which it would be impossible for strontium salts to perform.[1] Thus

---

[1] Whether a gradual adaptation to strontium salts could ever take place, or, in other words, whether in the course of many generations strontium-protein compounds could gradually be utilized like the corresponding calcium compounds, is an entirely different question. However, in this connection only the simpler kinds of organisms might yield satisfactory results. It may be mentioned that 0.1 per cent strontium nitrate added to the culture water does not, even after months, injure Diatoms, Flagellata, or Infusoria in presence of sufficient lime.

far the defenders of the metabolic theory have given no satisfactory explanation. The writer's above-mentioned theory on the function of lime salts, on the other hand, makes it perfectly clear why strontium salts in certain doses become hurtful and even poisonous for all organisms except the lowest forms of algæ and fungi.

POISONOUS ACTION OF MAGNESIUM SALTS.

If the writer's view that a calcium protein compound participates in the organized parts of the nucleus and chlorophyll body is correct, it might be expected that magnesium salts of the stronger acids would exert a noxious action. The lime as the stronger base would in such a case combine with the acid of the magnesium salt, while magnesia would enter into the place which the lime had occupied in the organized structures, the capacity for imbibition would thereby be altered, and a disturbance of the structure would result which would prove fatal. On the other hand, judging from the laws of the action of masses, it would naturally be inferred that an excess of lime salts would remedy the evil effects by making the reverse process possible. As a matter of fact, a detrimental action is observed when plants are treated with sulphate or nitrate of magnesium in the absence of calcium salts—an effect which is not observed when the same plants are exposed to the exclusive action of calcium, sodium, or potassium sulphate or nitrate. These phenomena were foreseen by the writer, and may be readily explained by his theory, while the holders of other views have not come forward with an explanation.

The writer observed that *Spirogyra* died within four to five days in a 1 per mille solution of magnesium sulphate, but remained alive for a long time in corresponding solutions of sodium, potassium, or calcium. In a 1 per cent solution of magnesium nitrate smaller kinds of *Spirogyra* will die in from six to twelve hours, but will live a long time in corresponding solutions of sodium, potassium, and calcium nitrate. *Spirogyra* which had been kept for several weeks in a healthy condition in a solution of 0.1 per mille of monopotassium phosphate in absolutely pure distilled water, died within three to four days when 2 per mille magnesium sulphate was added to this solution, but when dipotassium phosphate instead of the monophosphate was used death set in much later, that is, after fifteen to eighteen days.

Some threads of *Spirogyra majuscula* placed in a solution (1 liter) containing 0.02 per mille each of magnesium nitrate and ammonium sulphate, died in from ten to twelve days, while in the control solution, containing calcium nitrate in place of magnesium nitrate, they were still alive after six weeks, although cell division had stopped completely, and the cells exhibited an emaciated appearance owing to the absence of other mineral nutrients. In still another case threads of the same alga were placed in a solution of 1 per mille of magnesium nitrate, while in the control case 3 per mille of calcium nitrate was added.[1] In the former case death resulted in five days,[2] while in the latter the cells were still alive after a number of weeks. Lime salts, therefore, are the antidote for magnesium salts.[3] Nothing can replace them successfully in this case, not even nourishment with organic matter.[4] Microscopical examinations of *Spirogyra* cells exposed to the exclusive action of magnesium salts show that the nucleus is attacked first and then the chlorophyll body is injured, the phenomena closely resembling those produced by potassium oxalate, but while in a 1 per cent solution of magnesium sulphate the nucleus will swell up after twelve hours, in a 0.5 per cent solution of potassium oxalate it will do so in a much shorter time.

The noxious action of magnesium salts also soon becomes evident in the roots of seedlings. Thus *Vicia* and *Pisum* do not start lateral roots when kept in a solution of 0.5 per cent magnesium sulphate or nitrate, and the root cap and epidermal cells die after a few days. In a solution of calcium nitrate of equal strength, however, development continues. Seedlings of *Phaseolus* placed in a solution of 0.1 per cent magnesium sulphate, with 0.1 per cent monopotassium phosphate, showed injury to the roots after five days, and the entire plant succumbed soon afterwards. Similar observations had been made by Wolf, by Raumer and Kellerman, and by others, but all failed to recognize the true cause and to ascertain that lime salts alone act as the specific remedy.

Raumer[5] observed that in *Phaseolus multiflorus* kept in various culture solutions there was a detrimental effect much sooner when lime alone was absent than when both lime and magnesia were absent. The difference was most striking in the main roots and also in the number and vigor of the lateral roots. Here, then, the noxious effect of magnesia in the absence of lime is again manifested.

The writer has made a special study of the development of roots in culture solutions free from lime and from magnesia, using branches of *Tradescantia* for this purpose. These have calcium as well as magnesium salts stored up in their nodes, and hence some development of roots is possible even in distilled water. Nevertheless, a most striking difference was noticed, the roots in the culture solutions containing lime but not magnesia producing a "dense forest" of root hairs that reached a length of one-fourth centimeter, while the roots in solutions

[1] These observations the writer described in Flora, 1892, and also in Landw. Vers. Stat. of the same year.

[2] The time is probably prolonged when lime salts are stored up.

[3] An addition of strontium salts may delay death for a short period, but it can not prevent it, as do calcium salts.

[4] It may be mentioned that *Spirogyra* remains alive for from five to six weeks if kept in distilled water. Of course any further development is stopped, but assimilation and respiration soon reach a suitable equilibrium.

[5] Landw. Vers., 1883, Vol. XXIX, pp. 254 and 268.

containing magnesia but no lime, although larger than the others,[1] produced only a few short hairs. The lack of lime in these roots was felt especially in the epidermis, the interior parts being able to draw a sufficient amount of lime from the stem. Indeed, a microchemical test showed the presence of lime in the ash of these roots, gypsum needles forming when treated with a little sulphuric acid.

The extraordinary effects of lime salts on the development of root hairs is of special interest, as it furnishes the key to the observation of Wolff that the potassium and ammonium salts of the soil are absorbed in increased quantities by plants after manuring with lime salts.

LIFE WITHOUT LIME SALTS.

While lime salts are indispensable for animals, Phanerogams, and higher algæ, they are not so in the case of bacteria, fungi, and lower algæ. Thus far no investigations relating to the higher fungi have been made in this regard. The occurrence of lime in the ash of yeast or of tubercle bacilli[2] must be regarded as merely accidental. It was first observed by Adolph Mayer that for yeast magnesia is of greater importance than is lime. Later the writer proved that yeast and bacteria can do without lime entirely,[3] and Molisch has observed that this is also true of mold fungi.[4] It has been observed, on the other hand, that in certain cases the presence of lime promotes the action of fungi, but this is very probably due only to a secondary effect. Thus, the nitrification in soils is enhanced by calcium carbonate, and, according to Thaxter and Wheeler,[5] the scab of potatoes and of sugar beets is increased by liming the soil. Recently Laurent[6] reported that certain bacteria, *Bacillus coli communis* and *B. fluorescens putidus*, can attack potatoes in soils which have been strongly limed. He believes that by this means the power of resistance of these plants is diminished so much that the microbes named can commence their parasitic life, and

---

[1] These roots were 4.1 cm. long, while those in culture solutions without magnesia were only 3.2 cm. long. The composition of the complete culture solution in the above case was as follows:

	Per mille.
Monopotassium phosphate	0.1
Potassium nitrate	.5
Sodium sulphate	.2
Calcium nitrate	.5
Magnesium sulphate	.2
Ferrous sulphate	Trace.

[2] According to de Schweinitz and Dorsett (Centralbl. f. Bakt., No. 23, 1898), the phosphates of sodium, calcium, and magnesium predominate in this ash over that of potassium, while the reverse is true in the ash of yeast.

[3] Flora, 1892, pp. 374 and 390.

[4] Ber. Wien Akad., 1894, Vol. CIII.

[5] Storer, Relation of Agriculture, Vol. II, p. 546.

[6] Ann. de l'Institut Pasteur, 1899, Vol. XIII, p. 1.

he further asserts that only such plants can resist as have at the same time a great amount of potash and phosphoric acid.[1]

Both Molisch[2] and the writer[3] have observed that lime is not required by the lowe rforms of algæ. Molisch proved this in the case of *Ulothrix, Microthamnion, Stichococcus*, and *Protococcus*,[4] and the writer proved it in the case of a kind of *Palmella*.

Bipartition, zoospores, isogamy, and oogamy represent a scale of progress which probably requires an increasing differentiation of the nuclei. Isogamy in its simpler forms must be distinguished from its more perfected form, as it is found for instance in copulation of *Spirogyra*, where the uniting plasma bodies remain protected by the cellulose wall during the entire process. Some forms of the order *Protococcoideæ* multiply only by bipartition, others by swarm spores, certain forms by isogamy, but only two genera (*Volvox* and *Eudorina*[5]) by oogamy. In the order of the *Confervoideæ, Ulothrix* multiplies only by isogamy, while *Œdogonium* multiplies by oogamy also. In other groups a still higer potentialization of the nucleus has to be inferred, as in the *Characeæ* from the highly differentiated structure. Since neutral potassium oxalate has a poisonous effect upon *Diatoms, Œdogonium, Cladophora*, and apparently also on *Draparnaldia*, the presence of important lime compounds in these organisms may be inferred. All these organisms, however, are more differentiated than *Ulothrix*, which, according to Molisch, can grow in the absence of lime salts.

A careful study and comparison of the various chloroplasts of algæ might also show certain advantages in favor of those which require lime for their development. For instance, certain low genera, such as *Nostoc* and *Oscillaria*, form no starch, while others do. In such cases starch formation is to be regarded as a step forward, one that depends upon a higher differentiation of the chloroplasts. The beautiful chloroplasts of *Spirogyra* show a high degree of differentiation, the pyrenoids, which form stations in the chloroplasts, being the manufacturers of the starch.

It is true Schmitz also observed well-defined chloroplasts multiplying

---

[1] A satisfactory explanation as to the decrease of power of resistance under the influence of such an important nutrient as lime would be very desirable. Perhaps the cells beneath the lenticels are thereby stimulated to growth and open a way for the parasites to enter.

[2] Sitzungsber. d. Wiener. Akad. d. Wissenschaften, 1895, Vol. CIV. In this article Molisch has also proved that the algæ mentioned are incapable of assimilating free nitrogen. This confirms an earlier observation on *Nostoc* by the writer (Biol. Centralbl., Vol. X, p. 591) and a later observation by Kossowitsch.

[3] Botan. Centralbl., 1895, No. 52. Probably *Nostocaceæ* and *Oscillatoriaceæ* also do not require lime. The culture of *Oscillaria*, however, presents especial difficulties.

[4] It was not ascertained whether any other mode of multiplication than that by bipartition would be possible in the absence of lime in some of the forms mentioned. This question might also be raised in regard to fungi.

[5] It would be of special interest to ascertain whether *Eudorina* and *Volvox* require lime salts. They probably do.

by bipartition in such simple alga forms as *Protococcus, Stichococcus,* and *Palmella,* but these chloroplasts appear to be of a lower order than those of *Cladophora, Zygnema,* or *Spirogyra.*

The nutrition of the chloroplasts is in all probability cared for by the nucleus, hence it is reasonable to suppose that nuclei which prepare calcium-protein compounds for themselves furnish these same compounds to the chloroplasts also. This is probably the simplest explanation as to why chloroplasts become sensitive to even neutral oxalates in all plants the nuclei of which are killed by oxalates. Where the nuclei contain calcium-protein compounds the chloroplasts also contain them.

The writer has advanced the view that a higher development in form and function becomes possible only when the lower forms of life acquire the ability to assimilate lime and to utilize the resulting calcium proteid compound for organization purposes. This seems to him the simplest explanation of the fact that lime salts are required by all plants except the very lowest forms. Agreeing especially well with this view is the further observation that neither neutral oxalates, nor magnesium, nor strontium salts are injurious to these lowest forms,[1] although noxious to all other plant life.

If lime were necessary only for certain processes of metabolism in plants, as some authors claim, it would not only follow that the higher forms of algae have quite a different mode of metabolism from the lower ones, but it would also remain entirely incomprehensible why magnesium salts act so poisonously on the nucleus and why only calcium salts can prevent this deleterious effect. It would be very interesting to know the exact line of development below which calcium salts are not required and above which they are indispensable for plant life. A division of the algae into two such groups would certainly prove instructive.

ON POSSIBLE RELATIONS BETWEEN THE LIME AND THE TRANSPORTATION OF STARCH.

One of the first disturbances to appear when there is a deficiency of lime is the cessation of starch transportation. Starch gradually accumulates in the lower parts of the stem, and even its transportation from the storage receptacles to the axial parts may gradually stop. It has already been seen (p. 18) that a similar phenomenon was observed by Nobbe in plants showing a deficiency of chlorine compounds. Two causes, either separately or combined, may produce this phenomenon, and it follows, therefore, that the conditions bringing it on in different cases may not necessarily be wholly identical. One cause may be that cells fail to produce the diastase which is necessary for dissolving

---

[1] *Palmella* can develop quite well, even in 4 per cent solutions of neutral potassium oxalate or magnesium sulphate to which traces of ammonium sulphate and potassium phosphate had been added. Beer yeast may be kept for several hours at 30° C. in a 1 per cent solution of magnesium nitrate without serious injury.

the starch, and another the impossibility of forming in the growing parts new plastids and chloroplasts, which produce starch from sugar.

The writer's view, according to which lime is required in the compounds which build up nuclei and chromatophores, explains not only the failure to increase these organoids, but also that to produce diastase when lime is absent. Enzyms are secreted from the nuclei, as Hofer has shown with amœbæ, and therefore if the nuclei can not be normally formed for want of lime enzym formation also may stop. However, this latter explanation does not seem to apply for the initial pathological stage, since Raumer and Kellerman observed that in *Phaseolus multiflorus* sugar also was formed from starch for a certain period when lime was deficient, hence diastase was probably present.

In this case the upper part of the stem was devoid of starch and seemed to be incapable of forming starch from the sugar present. This accumulation of sugar prevented any further solution of starch in the lower parts.

The intensity of starch transportation depends essentially on two factors, (1) the saccharifying activity, and (2) the starch-forming activity of the plastids in other parts of the plants.

Further investigations in this direction would be very desirable. They would perhaps also show differences between the action of chlorids and that of lime in regard to the transportation of starch. Finally, since a deficiency of lime, like the absence of phosphoric acid, potassa, or magnesia, stops the formation of new cells, an accumulation of proteins may result, and indeed such a case was observed by Stock, the crystalloids increasing in number when lime was deficient.[1]

THE PHYSIOLOGICAL RÔLE OF MAGNESIUM SALTS.

It has already been pointed out that magnesium salts are especially important in the formation of seeds, but they are also required by all other parts of plants, and especially in the process of development. The amount of magnesia taken up by crops varies considerably. For example, an average crop of wheat will take up 8 kilos per hectare, a crop of leguminous plants 12 kilos, and a crop of tobacco as much as 43 kilos. It has also been pointed out that magnesium salts can fulfill their nourishing functions only in the presence of calcium salts, while in the absence of calcium salts they even exert an injurious action.[2]

In studying the questions as to what the nourishing function of magnesium salts is and why they can not be replaced physiologically by calcium salts, the probable answer is found in the well-known property of the magnesium salts to easily undergo dissociation, as the writer pointed out some years ago.[3] Magnesium salts are easily hydrolyzed, as is shown in the preparation of chlorid or carbonate of magnesium in the

---

[1] Bot. Centralbl., Vol. LIII, p. 83.
[2] Only the lowest algæ and fungi are exceptions (p. 44).
[3] Flora, 1892, p. 286.

ordinary method of preparation, whereby a part of the acid is easily liberated. Moreover, in boiling with water the secondary magnesium phosphate is decomposed into tertiary phosphate and free phosphoric acid. The inference suggests itself that this property is of great value to the cells, since in the assimilation of nitrogen from nitrates, sulphur from sulphates, and phosphoric acid from phosphates, the dissociation of these salts would immediately precede assimilation; hence the easier these acids are separated from the base the easier their assimilation will be accomplished. However, this deduction relates more to the assimilation of phosphoric acid than to that of sulphur and nitrogen. This latter assimilation must be possible also, to a certain degree, from other sulphates and nitrates besides those of magnesia. According to this view the formation of nucleo-proteids depends upon the presence of magnesium salts. As a matter of fact, it is found that magnesia always increases where rapid development is taking place. In accordance with this view also, very small quantities of magnesium salts can be used for a great deal of work, since the same amount of base can serve over and over again as the vehicle for assimilation of phosphoric acid. This may also explain the fact, pointed out long ago by Adolph Mayer, that "magnesia is more movable in the plant than lime is," and that "magnesia, like the phosphates, follows the proteids."

The fact that comparatively little magnesia can serve for extended physiological operations may be noticed in fungi in culture solutions devoid of lime, and also when seeds are left to develop in culture solutions free from magnesia and with only a moderate amount of lime in proportion to phosphoric acid. For example, beans may reach even 1 meter in height in such solutions, the reserve magnesia sufficing for this result.

Besides the easy dissociation the solubility of the secondary magnesium phosphate in water must also be considered. This solubility is much greater than that of the secondary calcium phosphate. When 100 cc. of a 0.2 per cent solution of disodium phosphate are mixed with 2 to 3 cc. of a 10 per cent solution of magnesium nitrate no precipitate is formed, while with an equivalent amount of calcium nitrate there will be a considerable precipitate. It may be inferred, therefore, that the secondary magnesium phosphate is more capable of migrating in plants than is the calcium phosphate, at least in neutral media and in the cytoplasm and its intercellular connections.

The alga *Spirogyra* is especially well adapted to show the influence of magnesium salts upon the production of protein matter. This influence may be double, (1) in facilitating the assimilation of sulphur and nitrogen from sulphates and nitrates the albumin formation as such is enhanced; and (2) in making the assimilation of phosphoric acid possible, nucleo-proteids may be formed, so that division of the nucleus and growth can proceed. If growth is as energetic as the formation of protein no accumulation of protein will take place, all being organized for the wants of the multiplying cells. However, by reducing the amount of phosphate to a trace multiplication can be very much retarded or stopped altogether, while albumin formation may go on; hence in this case an accumulation of albumin takes place either in the cell sap or in the cytoplasm or in both.

These conclusions can be very easily verified by studies with *Spirogyra*, for which the bicarbonate, obtained by dissolving magnesium carbonate in water charged with carbonic acid, is a very favorable form of magnesium. Thus a most energetic growth was observed with the following composition:

	Per mille.
Magnesium bicarbonate	0.5
Magnesium sulphate	.1
Calcium nitrate	.5
Monopotassium phosphate	.05
Potassium nitrate	.2
Ferrous sulphate	Trace.

The supposition that the favorable action of the magnesium bicarbonate consists simply in a "neutralization of acids" formed in the process of metabolism, can not be correct, since a substitution of an equal amount of calcium bicarbonate by no means shows the same beneficial influence, and besides in this case the above culture solution would contain such an excess of lime over magnesia that the assimilation of phosphoric acid might be retarded, involving a slower development.

The foregoing makes it intelligible why in the absence of magnesium salts the multiplication of cells is stopped, the nucleus not being able to increase to that point where division sets in. In the mixture of different salts occurring in plants there is sufficient opportunity for magnesia to combine with phosphoric acid, and the secondary magnesium phosphate thus formed can, in passing into the tertiary salt, yield some free acid. The tertiary salt remaining can easily be redissolved by weak organic acids, and thus yield again the secondary phosphate, which may in turn be utilized for the assimilation of phosphoric acid. This explains why germinating seeds and rapidly growing parts generally develop an acid reaction.

The rapidly proceeding cell division requires the most favorable conditions for the assimilation of phosphoric acid. One of these consists in utilizing the same amount of magnesia over and over again. Where an abundance of magnesium salts is present, however, as in most culture solutions of bacteria, the reaction does not need to be acid to insure a rapid assimilation of phosphoric acid.

Thus far few authors have expressed any view as to the primary functions of magnesia. Raumer observed that *Phaseolus multiflorus*, grown in culture solutions without magnesia, reached 1 meter in height, after which the internodes stopped stretching, but thickened abnormally. The new leaves also remained small and ceased to produce chlorophyll [1]—an interesting case of chlorosis, which disease may be

---

[1] Hoppe's chlorophyllan contains 0.34 per cent magnesia, but this product is now declared to be a mixture.

produced by other causes than by the absence of iron, as has been already pointed out (p. 15). Raumer ascribed to magnesia and not to lime, as Boehm has done, the transportation of starch, basing his claim on the ground that in the beginning the leaves contain not only considerable starch, but also a relatively large proportion of magnesia, which condition is found later in the stems. Finally, magnesia is found to be increased in the seeds, in which starch also is generally deposited. This hypothesis does not, however, seem to be well founded, since the relations indicated are not direct. Many other facts make it much more probable that it is the proteids and not the starch that have a close relation to magnesia. Where development is going on, starch is required for furnishing the necessary carbon and hydrogen in the production of proteids, hence magnesia is found in cases where the starch is migrating. Here magnesia is connected with the protein production and not with the migration of starch. Furthermore, the organoids of starch formation, the plastids, also require magnesium salts for their growth and multiplication, since they contain phosphoric acid in their nucleoproteids; hence there also exist some reasons for the belief in the remote connections between the starch content of an organ and the amount of magnesia present, but not in the direct connection supposed by Raumer.

INCREASE OF MAGNESIA IN OILY SEEDS.

If the writer's theory as regards the relation of magnesia to phosphoric acid is correct, more magnesia ought to be found where both compounds, nucleo-proteids as well as lecithin, are formed than where nucleo-proteids alone exist, since the assimilation of phosphoric acid is required not only for the formation of nucleo-proteids, such as chromatin and plastin, but also for that of lecithin. Lecithin is a constant concomitant of fat, and therefore seeds rich in fat ought to contain, cet. par., more magnesia than such as are rich in starch. A review of Wolff's ash tables confirms this deduction. The following table shows that for 1,000 parts of organized substance there are of magnesia in—

Starchy seeds.		Oily seeds.	
	Per cent.		*Per cent.*
Oats	1.9	Cotton	5.6
Barley	2	Flax	4.7
Rye	2	Poppy	4.9
Maize	1.9	Rape	4.6

The average proportion of magnesia in starchy seeds to that in oily seeds, therefore, is as 2 to 5.

It may furthermore be pointed out that fungi grown in culture solutions containing only traces of magnesia form no spores. Spores, however, contain lecithin, and in all probability relatively large amounts of nucleo-protein. Here the importance of magnesia can be readily demonstrated by increasing its amount in the culture solution, after which spores are soon formed. A similar effect on oats was observed by Schneidewind.[1] Of all nitrates tested, magnesium nitrate yielded the largest grain production.

NECESSITY OF MAGNESIUM SALTS FOR FUNGI.

Magnesium salts are also indispensable for fungi, but an exceedingly small amount will suffice when the nourishing solution has an acid reaction. In fact, even traces of magnesia taken up from glass vessels, if the latter are not made of the most resistant material, will suffice for growth. Fränkel denies the necessity of magnesia for certain kinds of bacteria—[2] *Bacterium coli*, *B. pyocyaneus* Friedl., and other bacteria having been cultivated by him in solutions of aspartate or lactate of ammonia in absence of magnesium salts. However, a suspicion as to the absolute purity of his materials may be justly entertained.

How small a quantity may suffice for mold fungi is shown by the following observation: The writer prepared a nourishing solution containing 2 per cent of ammonium acetate, 0.04 per cent monopotassium phosphate, and 0.02 per cent potassium sulphate and infected the solution, which was made with absolutely pure materials, with spores of *Penicillium*, but obtained no growth, owing to the absence of magnesia. He then added 0.0003 per cent of magnesium sulphate, and soon a considerable development of mycelium took place, its weight finally becoming very nearly the same as that in the control flask containing 0.1 per cent of magnesium sulphate.[3] The only difference observed between the two cases was that in the former flask spores were entirely absent, while in the latter they were present in great numbers.

Günther[4] inferred from his experiments that the limit of sensibility of the fungus *Rhizopus* to magnesium sulphate is 0.005 milligram. From such experiments it seems very probable that in those made by Fränkel with bacteria traces of magnesia were present as impurities in some of the compounds used.

Molisch has observed, and his observations have been confirmed by the writer, that spores of *Penicillium* do not even germinate in culture solutions entirely free from magnesia and containing ammonium acetate as the only organic nutrient—a fact which appears very strange, as there is certainly stored up in the spores a sufficient amount of magnesium phosphate to make germination and even some further development possible, and indeed magnesia has been found repeatedly in the ash of various fungi. The writer has cultivated *Penicillium* in a solution containing peptone, tartaric acid, monopotassium phosphate, and 0.1 per cent magnesium sulphate, and has convinced himself of the

---

[1] Journ. f. Landw., 1898, Vol. XLVI, p. 1.
[2] Centralbl. f. Bakt., Vol. XVII, p. 32.
[3] Experiments with *Penicillium* succeed best in moderately acid solutions.
[4] Loc. cit. (p. 25).

presence of magnesia in the spores.[1] However. these same spores did not germinate in the solution of ammonium acetate used by Molisch and by the writer, but they germinated in various other solutions, as, for instance, in a 0.5 per cent solution of sodium acetate or of cane sugar containing a small amount of ammonium sulphate. It appears probable, therefore, that a solution containing ammonium acetate as sole organic nutrient is unfavorable for starting in the spores certain processes which render the stored-up magnesium phosphate available for the beginning of germination. Perhaps there is formed in the spores the but little soluble magnesium ammonium phosphate when too much ammonia is present in the culture solution. In suitable culture solutions, free of magnesia, the magnesium phosphate stored up in the spores may be economically utilized, and even a considerable mass of mycelium may be produced provided an abundant sowing of spores had taken place.

CAN MAGNESIUM SALTS BE REPLACED BY BERYLLIUM SALTS?

The attempts to penetrate the mystery of the physiological functions of magnesium naturally have raised the question whether beryllium can perform the functions of magnesium in living cells, since the general behavior of the compounds of these elements bears a strong chemical resemblance to each other.

In 1890 Sestini[2] undertook to determine whether wheat could be raised in culture solutions in which magnesium sulphate was replaced by beryllium sulphate. He sowed the grains in quartz sand which had been treated with hydrochloric acid to remove all mineral impurities, and watered the plants with a culture solution containing beryllium sulphate in place of magnesium sulphate. The plants reached a height of 90 to 95 cm., but the control experiment showed the superiority of magnesium over beryllium, as will be seen by the following comparison:

Wheat grown—	Number of seeds.	Weight of seeds.	Weight of single seed.
		Grams.	*Grams.*
In the beryllium solution	283	12.31	0.435
In the magnesium solution	322	15.20	.472

[1] It has been shown by Aso that the spores of *Aspergillus* contain a moderate amount of magnesia. He has kindly furnished the writer the results of an analysis which yielded for the ash of spores of *Aspergillus oryzae* the following composition:

	Per cent.
Potassa	45.96
Soda	4.13
Lime	1.03
Magnesia	4.36
Oxid of iron	4.91
Phosphoric acid	39.64
Sulphuric acid	2.00
Silica	.40

The percentage of ash in the dry matter was 5.15. The fungus had been grown on boiled rice.

[2] Le Staz. Agr. Ital., Vol. XX; Centralbl. f. Agr. Chem., 1890, p. 464, and 1891, p. 558.

The harvested seeds were grown again in the same way.[1] Of twenty seeds of the plants grown in beryllium solution, however, only seven germinated and only three of the plants produced seeds, the resulting crop of fourteen seeds weighing only 0.37 gram and averaging only 0.026 gram. This clearly shows that beryllium can not replace magnesium in wheat, and very probably also not in any other of the Phanerogams. The fact that the first generation yielded a much better result than the second must be ascribed to the presence of a relatively large amount of magnesium phosphate in the seeds used.

In an experiment made by the writer with shoots of *Tradescantia* placed in culture solutions containing 0.1 per cent beryllium sulphate in one case and 0.1 per cent magnesium sulphate in the other, the lower leaves of the beryllium plant commenced to die after several weeks, and the newly developed upper leaves scarcely reached one-third the normal size, these shoots dying off after eight weeks, while in the control case they were still in a healthy condition.[2]

In regard to algæ, the writer has observed that a solution of beryllium sulphate in which the other mineral nutrients are wanting exercises an injurious influence sooner than does the magnesium sulphate. Some threads of *Spirogyra communis* were placed in 0.2 per cent of these salts dissolved in purest distilled water, and it was found that the number of dead and injured cells was much larger after two days in the former case than in the latter.[3]

In a subsequent experiment the amount of both these sulphates was diminished and mineral nutrients added, the composition of the main solution being—

	Per mille.
Calcium nitrate	0.10
Calcium sulphate	.01
Monopotassium phosphate	.01
Dipotassium phosphate	.01
Beryllium sulphate	.10

In this solution *Spirogyra* threads were still normal and healthy after three weeks, but had not grown to any noticeable extent.

In another experiment the following solution was prepared:

	Per mille.
Calcium nitrate	0.25
Calcium sulphate	.10
Monopotassium carbonate	1.00
Monopotassium phosphate	.05
Ferrous sulphate	Trace.

One half of this solution received 0.2 gram magnesium sulphate and the other half 0.2 gram beryllium sulphate. Very soon a slight turbidity, followed later by a flocculent precipitate, was noticed in the beryl-

---

[1] The ash of the beryllium plants contained 2 per cent of BeO.

[2] Mineral nutrients are stored up in the nodes, as already mentioned.

[3] For further information relative to the noxious effect of magnesium salts in absence of calcium see p. 42.

lium solution, while the control solution remained absolutely clear. Into both flasks a trace of a *Palmella* culture, with some Diatoms, was now introduced. After four weeks it was found that the Diatoms had multiplied to a great extent in the control solution, but not one could be observed after repeated microscopical examinations in the beryllium solution. The *Palmella,* however, was well developed in both flasks. This might seem to indicate that such a simple alga form as *Palmella* could utilize beryllium salts in place of magnesium salts, at least when it is offered in a favorable culture solution, but slight traces of magnesia might have been furnished by the glass vessel.

To determine the effects of beryllium on fungi an experiment was made by Molisch, the culture solution used containing—

	Poc mille.
Ammonium acetate	20. 00
Beryllium sulphate	.40
Monopotassium phosphate	.04
Ferrous sulphate	.01

There was no development whatever in this solution when spores of *Penicillium* were inoculated, but upon the addition of 0.02 per cent magnesium sulphate 78 milligrams of fungous mass was produced after nineteen days.

Notwithstanding the close chemical relations between beryllium and magnesium there must exist such chemical differences that the inability of beryllium to physiologically replace magnesium can be easily explained. As the text-books on chemistry fail to give minute comparisons of the chemical behavior of soluble beryllium and magnesium salts toward phosphates, the writer has made a few tests in this regard. When 1 per mille solutions of beryllium sulphate and dipotassium phosphate are mixed the liquid is at first clear at the ordinary temperature, but gradually becomes opalescent, and after one day the beryllium is precipitated as a flocculent phosphate, but if the mixture is heated or if some sodium acetate is added a flocculent precipitate is produced at once. Magnesium sulphate behaves very differently, giving no precipitate whatever under the same conditions.

If a 10 per cent solution of monopotassium phosphate is mixed with a 10 per cent solution of magnesium sulphate no precipitate is formed at the ordinary temperature, and the liquid remains clear even on boiling. This, however, is not the case with beryllium sulphate, which produces a copious flocculent precipitate in a few minutes, and even if more dilute solutions, as for example a 1 per cent solution of monopotassium phosphate and beryllium sulphate, are mixed the mixture becomes turbid on boiling.

Although a higher diluted solution of beryllium sulphate gives no precipitate with monopotassium phosphate, the addition of sodium acetate, even at the ordinary temperature, will cause a precipitate of beryllium phosphate. Thus even in a dilution of 0.001 per cent beryllium sulphate, turbidity will be produced and finally some flocculi will be deposited. Under the same condition solutions of magnesium sulphate, whether highly or moderately diluted, will remain perfectly clear.

It is seen, therefore, that there is a fundamental difference between beryllium and magnesium salts in their behavior to phosphoric acid—a difference which amply accounts for the fact that beryllium salts can not replace magnesium salts, as far as the process of the assimilation of phosphoric acid is concerned. In this respect magnesium is unrivaled even by the most closely related elements. With the properties of easy dissociation of the salts and its character as only a weak base, magnesia unites a moderate solubility of the secondary phosphate not found with any other related base. Although beryllium oxid is also a weak base, the fact that it is much more inclined than magnesia to yield an insoluble phosphate renders it unsuitable for the function mentioned.

As to the rarer elements it may still be questioned whether there may not exist among them some that could physiologically replace magnesium or calcium. The experiments with cerium and lanthanium showed no evidence in favor of that view, these salts killing algæ in a solution of 0.1 per cent. Thorium sulphate is not so injurious, but no further studies as to whether it can be utilized for any physiological function have been made, nor have any experiments been made with yttrium, niobium, or some other rare elements.

IMPORTANCE OF LIME SALTS FOR ANIMALS.

In animals lime salts are necessary not simply for the formation of the bones, but also for every part of the body, and they are required for the lowest forms as well as for the higher animals.

The action of the heart is above all most intimately connected with the presence of lime salts. Thus, a frog's heart will soon stop even in a physiologic salt solution (0.6 per cent sodium chloride), but will continue to beat when some ash of blood is dissolved in the same solution. Ringer has shown that a good circulating fluid for the heart may be compounded by preparing a mixture of such salts as normally occur in the blood. In such a solution the isolated frog's heart will beat almost as long as it would in defibrinated blood. Halliburton[1] says: "The necessity for lime salts is especially great. In fact, the close adhesion of proteids generally with small quantities of mineral matter is rather suggestive of combination than mere mixture. Lime salts adhere especially closely and in fact seem indispensable for many of the functions of the body, of which the beating of the heart and the contraction of skeletal muscle are good examples. Blood from which the salts have been removed keeps the heart going, but the tracing is abnormal, resembling that produced by a weak solution of a lime salt. It is in

---

[1] Chem. Physiol., 1891, London, p. 256.

fact found that dialysis will not remove the lime from serum albumin, though it removes the greater part of the sodium and potassium salts."

The great importance of calcium salts for the various organs of animals is also illustrated by the empirical knowledge gained by physicians. Thus a prominent medical work[1] states: "Calcium chlorid is used with benefit as an internal remedy in the various manifestations of the strumous diathesis. It often causes the resolution of glandular enlargements and the calcification of tubercular deposits, aids the cicatrization of ulcerating cavities, and has proved curative in eczema and lupus. It is highly praised in phthisis, also in chorea, and for the colliquative diarrhœa of strumous children. In solution used externally as a fomentation it is said to hasten the maturation of boils." In direct contact with the heart, however, this salt is not harmless, as shown by the experiments with a frog's heart. Probably a hydrolytic dissociation, with liberation of hydrochloric acid, however slight it might be, brings on the injurious effect.[2]

Munk[3] observed during the inanition of men and dogs a gradual increase of the lime secreted in the urine. Katsuyama[4] noticed in observations on starving rabbits in the first four days a gradual decrease and afterwards a slow increase of lime in the urine, while there was a gradual and steady decrease of magnesia. This decrease of magnesia, compared with the increase of lime, is very significant and instructive.[5]

PROPORTIONS OF LIME AND MAGNESIA IN ANIMAL ORGANISMS.

The muscle fibrillæ of the mammalia are made up principally of the contractile substance, or, as Kupffer has called it, the dynamoplast. The energide (the nucleus with its connected cytoplasm), which manufactures the fibrillæ, occupies but a small volume within the dynamoplast, hence the writer's hypothesis would suggest the inference that the lime content of muscular masses should be less than that of glandular masses, since the relative mass of the nucleus in muscles is much smaller than in glands. From Katz's analyses the following data will show how far this view is confirmed.[6]

[1] Potter, O. L., Handbook of Materia Medica, Pharmacy, and Therapeutics, Philadelphia.

[2] Calcium hydrate introduced in man or dog tends to the secretion of calcium carbamate in the urine, as Abel has demonstrated. This is of special physiological interest, since carbamic acid is the precursor of urea, as Nencki and Drechsel have shown.

[3] Suppl. zu Virchow's Arch., Vol. CLI.

[4] Zeitsch. f. Phys. Chem., 1899, Vol. XXVI.

[5] It may be pointed out here that lime compounds also seem to play an important rôle in the coagulation of the blood, as this can be prevented by the addition of some soluble oxalate. Myosin, which possibly plays a part in the coagulation of the muscular plasm, also contains lime. Moreover the actions of rennet and of pectase are connected with the presence of lime.

[6] Pflüg. Arch., Vol. LXIII, p. 1.

There were found in 1,000 parts of fresh muscle of a—

	Part calcium.
Dog	0.0685
Hog	.0806
Deer	.0959
Cat	.0846
Man	.0748

or an average of 0.0809 part calcium. On the other hand Oidtman[1] found in the liver, the largest gland in mammalia, 0.284 part of calcium for 1,000 parts, or nearly three and a half times as much as the average in the muscle.

Embryos and young animals show a higher percentage of nuclear mass in the muscles than do full-grown animals, hence the fact that the muscles of the calf contain more lime than those of the cow[2] is in full accord with the writer's inference. Zoologists have further observed that the muscles of fishes and batrachia are relatively richer in nuclear mass than are those of mammalia. The fact that Katz[3] has found two to three times as much lime in the muscles of such animals as in those of mammalia is therefore strictly in accord with the writer's view. There is in 1,000 parts of fresh muscle of the—

	Parts calcium.
Frog	0.1566
Shad	.2206
Eel	.3913

or an average of 0.2562 part calcium.

The importance of lime for the division of cells even in the lower animal organisms is shown by Herbst's statement[4] that the most important salt for the development of the sea urchin's eggs is calcium phosphate, in the absence of which not even the completion of segmentation is possible. The calcium of this salt is just as important as the phosphoric acid. It happens that this salt is present in the sea water in very small quantities only, hence it must be assumed that these eggs have a great absorptive power for it.

A relative increase of magnesia can be observed in certain organs in which the nuclear mass is small. Thus, according to Geogehan, the human brain contains about ten times as much magnesium phosphate as calcium phosphate, and the muscles of mammalia contain in most cases more magnesia than those of batrachia and fishes, as shown by Katz's results.[5]

---

[1] Prize Treatise, Würzburg, 1858. This author found 1.1 per cent inorganic substance in the liver, and in 100 parts of this ash 3.62 per cent of lime and 0.19 per cent of magnesia. Calculating from these data, there are contained 0.2842 part of calcium and 0.0125 part of magnesium in 1,000 parts of fresh liver.

[2] The lime content of the liver cells is also larger, according to Krüger (1895), in the calf than in the cow, which suggests the necessity of further microscopic comparison as to the relative size of the nuclei.

[3] Loc. cit.

[4] Arch. f. Entwicklungsmechanik, Vol. V, p. 667.

[5] Loc. cit.

There is in 1,000 parts of fresh muscle of the—

	Part magnesium.
Dog	0.2370
Hog	.2823
Deer	.2906
Cat	.2863
Man	.2116
Average	.2611

while there is in 1,000 parts of fresh muscle of the—

	Part magnesium.
Frog	0.2353
Shad [1]	.1670
Eel	.1782
Average	.1935

A comparison of the averages shows for the—

	Calcium.	Magnesium.	Calcium.	Magnesium.
Muscles of mammalia	1 :	3.23 or	0.31	: 1
Muscles of frogs and fish	1 :	.75 or	1.33	: 1
Liver of mammalia	1 :	.04 or	25.00	: 1

Since it is seen that glands contain more calcium than muscles, and that the muscles of lower animals contain more calcium than those of the higher animals, one can not help seeking for a law underlying these facts, which are in full accord with the writer's inference t h a t t h e a m o u n t o f l i m e m u s t i n c r e a s e w i t h t h a t o f t h e n u c l e a r m a s s. On the other hand the high lecithin content of the brain may have a connection with the relative increase of magnesia in it (p. 50.)

It would be very interesting to analyze the gray and the white substances of the brain separately, as they show a great quantitative difference in the nuclear masses. Moreover, the peripheral nerve threads being poorest in nuclear mass. should also be investigated in this respect. It is regrettable that so far no physiologist has undertaken the work.[2]

BEHAVIOR OF ANIMALS TO STRONTIUM SALTS AND OXALATES.

The replacement of calcium salts by strontium salts is just as impossible in animals as in plants (p. 39). Not even in the formation of the bones can strontium phosphate take the place of calcium phosphate. Craemer fed a rapidly growing young dog for several months with food poor in lime, and to which an addition of strontium phosphate was made, and as a result great softness of the bones and rhachitic alterations were soon obvious. Weiske[3] arrived at the same conclusions and refuted the contrary opinions of Papillion and König. In the presence

---

[1] The unusually large proportion, 0.3102 part, found by Katz in the pike, may possibly be due to an error.

[2] The gray substance of the brain is richer in nuclear mass than the white substance and therefore ought to contain more lime.

[3] Zeitsch. f. Biol., Vol. XIII, p. 421.

of sufficient lime the poisonous action of strontium salts upon animals is weak.

The writer's hypothesis as to the functions of lime salts makes the poisonous action of soluble oxalates upon animals also more intelligible than it has been heretofore. The chief property of oxalates is to transform the calcium of calcium compounds into calcium oxalate. If therefore the nuclei of the cells contain calcium protein compounds in their organized structure, the removal of this calcium and its replacement by the sodium or potassium of the oxalate applied must alter the capacity of imbibition and thus cause fatal disturbances of the organized structure (tectonic). Indeed, oxalates constitute a general poison for all kinds of animals.[1] The writer has demonstrated that in a 0.5 per cent solution of neutral potassium or sodium oxalate *Rotatoria*, *Copepoda*, and aquatic *Asellids* die in thirty to fifty minutes, leeches and *Planaria* succumb a little later, and finally *Ostracodes* and larvæ of insects are killed. *Infusoria*, *Flagellata*, and *Amoebæ* were found to be dead in this solution after fifteen hours. Even a 0.1 per cent solution of sodium oxalate will kill some of the organisms named, such as *Copepoda* and *Rotatoria*. The poisonous action for vertebrates was known long ago, but the explanations were not entirely satisfactory. Some authors sought the cause in the obstruction of the vessels of the kidneys with calcium oxalate and in inflammation of the kidneys, and others believed in a decomposition of the oxalic acid with the production of the poisonous carbonic oxid, but the irritation and the final paralysis of the vasomotoric center pointed plainly to another cause.[2]

FINAL REMARKS.

The writer's deliberations have led him to conceive the probable rôle of calcium and magnesium salts in the living cells. This view is in full accord with various facts for which in former times no satisfactory explanation was reached.

It is now clear why magnesium is more movable in plants than calcium, and further, why the calcium content increases with the mass of nuclear substance and of chlorophyll bodies, and why magnesium salts increase wherever phosphoric acid is in increased demand for the production of lecithin and nuclein. It also makes it perfectly clear why on the one hand magnesium salts become poisonous in the absence of calcium salts, and why on the other hand the absence of magnesium salts in an otherwise complete culture solution leads to a gradual stoppage of all further development, and to final inanition. The formation of the nuclei and plastids requires calcium as well as magnesium salts,

---

[1] Noxious effects on the bones and kidneys and sometimes on the activity of the heart have been noticed after feeding cattle with vegetables containing soluble oxalates, such as leaves of the sugar beet.

[2] The fact that badly healing sores are produced when open wounds come in contact with oxalate solutions, a fact long known to photographers, deserves particular mention.

the former for the production of calcium nucleo-proteids and the latter for making possible the assimilation of phosphoric acid. If lime salts are in great excess in a neutral medium, the formation of magnesium phos phate and consequently the assimilation of phosphoric acid will be retarded, since the lime as the stronger base will withhold phosphoric acid when soluble phosphates come in contact with lime salts. Many plants, therefore, which have absorbed too much lime and relatively too little magnesia from the soil precipitate a part of the lime in the form of oxalate. Indeed Monteverde[1] observed that the amount of oxalic acid increases with the amount of lime absorbed.

The excess of lime is in reality the cause of an increased production of oxalic acid—a fact best explained by the assumption that before car bonic acid is finally produced by the combustion of carbohydrates, a series of organic acids, of which oxalic acid is one stage, is rapidly passed, this stage being fixed by the presence of lime. Similar obser vations were also made by Wehmer with fungi in culture solutions to which lime salts were added. In the presence of lime salts there was more oxalic acid formed than in its absence, or, more correctly expressed, more was preserved from being again destroyed by further oxidation.

The fact that seeds generally contain much more magnesia than lime may be considered an interesting case of adaptation. A rapid develop ment by an easy assimilation of the reserve phosphoric acid is thus assured—a favorable circumstance, as it lessens the danger of the mold ing and putrefying of the seeds sown in moist ground. The same plant after it develops chlorophyll, however, requires more lime in proportion to magnesia than does the seedling in its early stages. According to Wolff's calculations of the minima of lime and magnesia for oats there is required 0.2 per cent of each for the dry matter, but for plants with more abundant foliage the minimum of lime would be larger.

The proportion of these two constituents in the soils is a more potent factor in the resulting crop than is generally supposed. The many contradictory statements in regard to the influence of magnesia in the soils are easily explained by the aid of the above theory. A soil rich in magnesia will be damaged by liming with magnesian limestone, since this would increase still more the already large amount of magne sia, while a soil very poor in magnesia may be benefited by it. In the application of kainit and carnallit also the magnesia content of these potassa fertilizers has to be considered and eventually liming has to be carried on in conjunction with it.

---

[1] Bot. Jahresb. f. 1890, p. 75.

www.ingramcontent.com/pod-product-compliance
Lightning Source LLC
Chambersburg PA
CBHW022032080426
42733CB00007B/810